Growing Musicians

GROWING MUSICIANS
Teaching Music in Middle School and Beyond

Bridget Sweet

OXFORD
UNIVERSITY PRESS

OXFORD
UNIVERSITY PRESS

Oxford University Press is a department of the University of Oxford. It furthers
the University's objective of excellence in research, scholarship, and education
by publishing worldwide. Oxford is a registered trade mark of Oxford University
Press in the UK and certain other countries.

Published in the United States of America by Oxford University Press
198 Madison Avenue, New York, NY 10016, United States of America.

© Oxford University Press 2016

First Edition published in 2016

Library of Congress Cataloging-in-Publication Data
Sweet, Bridget, author.
Growing musicians : teaching music in middle school and beyond / Bridget Sweet.
pages cm
Includes bibliographical references and index.
ISBN 978-0-19-937206-5 (cloth : alk. paper)—ISBN 978-0-19-937207-2 (pbk. : alk. paper)
1. School music—Instruction and study—United States.   2. Middle schools—United States.
I. Title.
MT1.S949 2015
780.71'2—dc23
2015017982

For Jason, Luke, and Evelyn

You are the absolute loves of my life.

CONTENTS

PREFACE

Even as kids reach adolescence, they need more than ever for us to watch over them. Adolescence is not about letting go. It's about hanging on during a very bumpy ride. (Ron Taffel)

When I graduated from college with my bachelor's degree and certification in music education, I proclaimed, "*I am going to be a high school choir teacher!*" To me, that was it—go big or go home. However, my intentions fell victim to circumstance, and I found that my two choices for employment were either to build a K–12 music program from scratch within a small, rural community or to work as a junior high choral music teacher shared between two urban schools. In an effort to maintain the most secondary focus possible, I accepted the junior high choral position and kicked off the school year two days later. *No matter, as I would soon be a high school choir teacher.*

In the midst of my first year as a junior high music educator, my former high school choir teacher encouraged me to apply for the posted middle school position in my home district, placing me in alignment to succeed her following her imminent retirement. It was *perfect*. I would bide my time in the middle school until I could step into my dream job at the high school. Therefore, my second year as a music teacher began at Kenneth T. Beagle Middle School in Grand Ledge, Michigan. *I can see the light at the end of the tunnel! Soon I will be a high school choir teacher!*

John Lennon wrote in his song "Beautiful Boy," "Life is what happens to you while you're busy making other plans." While continuing to teach full time at Beagle Middle School, I began my Master of Music Education degree at Michigan State University (MSU) and completed my degree over summer and fall semesters. The combination of my class work at MSU and my work as a middle school choral teacher resulted in a greater appreciation for middle school students. I found that I took pleasure in the students' goofiness and quirkiness, and how every day was different and slightly unpredictable. I appreciated that I could be a powerful influence in my students' lives and reap the benefits of their youth and willingness to be silly. I enjoyed not "living in a fishbowl" with regard to public perception of my music program, as high school choral teachers sometimes experience. I immensely enjoyed how free I felt to be myself with middle school students—my own goofiness and quirkiness fell right in step with theirs. As a result, my interest in remaining with middle school students grew stronger than my interest in eventually taking over the high school choral position. Following graduation from the MSU master's degree program in 2003, I was urged to pursue a doctorate in music education. However, at that time I had no interest in leaving my position at Beagle Middle School to be a full-time student.

In the winter of 2005, a conversation with a high school choral teacher who had completed his Ph.D. in music education at MSU *while* teaching full-time rekindled my interest to pursue a doctoral degree. I decided that an eventual sabbatical from Beagle Middle School would allow me to complete my one-year residency requirement for a Ph.D., from which I could return to Beagle Middle School and continue teaching. The best of both worlds! I began my doctoral degree at MSU in the summer of 2005.

For the first two years of my doctoral program, I continued to teach full-time at the middle school. I found that my role as a middle school teacher meshed with that of a doctoral student and developing researcher, and I became strongly aware of a lack of research about, and advocates for, adolescent singers. As a result, my research focus shifted from the perspective of middle school students (as it had been throughout work on my master's degree) to the perspective of *teachers* of middle school students. What could we learn from exemplary middle school choir teachers to share with preservice teachers, developing teachers, and experienced teachers to assist them in facilitation of student-centered middle school choir classes based on democratic principles of music teaching and learning? This question led to the development of my dissertation (Sweet 2008), as well as to my resignation as the choir teacher at Beagle Middle School in order to complete my Ph.D. and pursue a collegiate music education position. During the final year of my degree program, I embraced life as a full-time doctoral student and prepared to answer this question in order to promote awareness of middle school choir students and develop advocates for this population.

Middle school students truly seem to be "my people." I feel a strong connection with their musical and personal needs and development, as well as their sense of humor. As previously mentioned, throughout my undergraduate degree program I considered teaching high school to be the pinnacle of the music education profession and anything else was, to my mind, less prestigious. Today, as a teacher of music educators, I see that version of myself in my students every semester of every year: young adults completely fixed on their futures as high school band, orchestra, or choral teachers. Regardless of where they land and whom they ultimately teach, I am honored to support and teach them and to provide opportunities for growth and reflection as they navigate the transition from student to teacher. However, I do find great enjoyment in educating my college students in the ways and joys of working with adolescents, which includes dissipating fears about puberty and fending off their own bad memories from middle school.

There is no precise span of years to define "adolescence." However, there is general agreement that the emotional, psychological, and physical transitions of adolescence can span from upper elementary school through high school and into adulthood. By looking beyond grade levels and focusing on developmental characteristics, I have developed an affinity for adolescents, whose unpredictability and sense of humor never fail to fascinate and amuse me, and whose journeys from childhood to adulthood never fail to intrigue and concern me. I recognize the potential power of middle-level music classes, from general music to ensemble participation, and believe that teaching methodologies and practices rooted in a safe and structured learning environment truly allow students to empower themselves *while* developing their musicianship.

ADDITIONAL VOICES

Although my middle school teaching background is rooted in choral music, this book is intended for all disciplines of middle school music teaching—choral, instrumental (band and orchestra), and general music. Throughout the book you will find commentary from middle school music teachers whom I interviewed about their work with adolescent music students. A constructivist approach helped me to examine how these middle school music teachers perceive and construct their own reality within a variety of teaching settings. As defined by Michael Crotty (1998):

> Constructivism points out the unique experience of each of us. It suggests that each one's way of making sense of the world is as valid and worthy of respect than any other, thereby tending to scotch any hint of a critical spirit. (Crotty 1998, 58)

I contacted colleagues at universities across the United States to gather names of exemplary choral, general music, band, and orchestra teachers. Colleagues provided a total of twenty-eight names and, following initial contact, sixteen teachers agreed to participate in my research. I have also included the insights of Deb Borton in this book, who was the primary participant of my dissertation.

Interviews took place either in person, over the telephone, or via Skype. Although each participant answered the same questions, interviews ranged from fifty to a hundred minutes in length, depending on the time each participant took to answer the questions. Each interview was digitally recorded and then transcribed, with a transcription provided to the respective interviewee to ensure accuracy and trustworthiness. The teachers answered follow up questions via email.

It is important to emphasize that my sharing of these teachers' perspectives and stories is not to claim their thinking as right or wrong, but rather to provide a variety of perspectives from which the reader may glean ideas, validation, and encouragement in working with adolescent musicians. Professor Michael Quinn Patton wrote in his 2002 book *Qualitative Research and Evaluation Methods* that, through examination of different perspectives, "the constructionist evaluator ... would not pronounce which set of perceptions was 'right' or more 'true' or more 'real'" (Patton 2002, 98). Thus, as he suggests, it is up to the reader to decide which of the discussed ideas, approaches, or philosophies best mesh with their own.

At the time of our interviews, the seventeen participants primarily taught middle school choir, band, strings, and general music; two of the teachers additionally taught guitar classes and/or a guitar ensemble. Because all of these middle school teachers differed in years of teaching experience, school settings, and teaching responsibilities, the following short biographies situate each person within his or her own teaching context. However, please keep in mind that these details indicate where each person was teaching at the time of data collection. Several of the teachers are no longer currently working at the school identified below; updated biographies can be found in Appendix A. Actual teacher names and school names are used throughout this book, unless a pseudonym was requested.

Deb Borton

Deb is a middle school teacher in Okemos, Michigan with a focus on choral music.

Bethany Cann

Bethany is a general music teacher at Penn Treaty Middle School in Philadelphia, Pennsylvania.

Robyn Chair (a pseudonym)

Robyn is an orchestra teacher at two middle schools and two elementary schools in Illinois.

Jay Champion

Jay teaches chorus, general music, and electronic music composition at Lost Mountain Middle School in Kennesaw, Georgia.

James Cumings

James is the middle school choir teacher at Kidder Middle School in Jackson, Michigan.

Matthew Dethrow

Matthew is a middle school teacher at Kennedy Junior High School in Lisle, Illinois with a focus on band.

Jason Freeland

Jason is the middle school band teacher at Central Middle School in Tinley Park, Illinois; he also teaches general music one hour per day.

Seth Gardner

Seth is a middle school teacher at Haverford Township Middle School in Havertown, Pennsylvania with a focus on choral music.

Sean Grier

Sean is one of the two choir teachers at the Durham School of the Arts (DSA) in Durham, North Carolina.

Michelle Limor Herring

Michelle is a middle school teacher at Lamar Middle School in Austin, Texas with a focus on choral music.

David Hirschorn

David teaches choral music and guitar at Durham Middle School in Cobb County, Georgia.

Michael Lehman

Michael is the middle school band teacher at Edison Middle School in Champaign, Illinois.

Marsha Miller (a pseudonym)

Marsha is a middle school teacher at Philip East Middle School in Illinois with a focus on band.

Andrew Nickles

Andrew teaches at Gridley Middle School within the Tucson Unified School District in Tucson, Arizona where he has integrated his string orchestras with his guitar ensembles.

Gretchen Pearson

Gretchen is a middle school teacher in Illinois with a focus on orchestra.

Kate Tyler (a pseudonym)

Kate is a general music teacher in Illinois and also teaches a middle school choir one day per week after school.

Tavia Zerman

Tavia is the middle school band teacher at Hayes Middle School in Grand Ledge, Michigan.

More than anything, middle school pulls in children and pitches back teenagers. It is a time of change, which means, at this age, many things. (Perlstein 2003, 6)

Each chapter in this book is designed to address different facets of working with adolescent music students. As will be discussed throughout, there is no single, clear-cut way to define or explain adolescent actions or thinking because each student progresses through adolescence at his or her own pace; nor is there just one way to teach adolescent music students. That said, this book will provide a variety of perspectives and considerations on which to reflect with regard to your own work as a music educator.

Chapter 1 provides foundational information and focuses on characteristics of young adolescents, ranging from physiological, emotional, and social development to identity development and self-esteem. As chapter 1 specifically focuses on the adolescent music student, chapter 2 concentrates on the music teacher. Conversation in chapter 2 addresses the development of our individual philosophies of teaching adolescent musicians and the varied roles that a music teacher plays in the lives of young adolescents. Within chapter 3, discussion centers on the music classroom climate, including acknowledgment of student diversity and cultivation of the music classroom as a safe place. Chapter 4 is focused on the equilibrium of flexibility and structure in a music program, as well as matters of classroom management, discipline, and bullying in the music classroom. Ideas of humanity and empathy are explored within chapter 5, as they are easily situated within the context of an adolescent music class. Humor is the overarching topic of chapter six—specifically, humor as a teaching tactic with adolescent musicians. When used mindfully, humor can be an effective and powerful teaching tool.

ACKNOWLEDGMENTS

The ideas within this book have been rattling around in my head, heart, and soul for a very long time. It has been quite an adventure exploring and embracing these ideas over the past years, and it is thrilling to see this project realized. So many people have assisted me along the way—truly an endeavor of this magnitude is never done alone. However, there are four main people who influenced my contemplation of the ideas contained in this book and, in varied ways, very much contributed to the formation of this book. I would like to acknowledge them in chronological order.

I know the first moment that I ever contemplated the idea of empowerment of adolescent musicians was during a doctoral advising meeting with my co-dissertation chairs, Dr. Sandra Snow and Dr. Mitchell Robinson, at Michigan State University. As we hashed out topics for my dissertation research, the two of them wholeheartedly encouraged me to study with middle school choir teacher, Deb Borton. I distinctly remember them saying, "If we could bottle and sell what Deb is doing over there with those middle school students. . . ." It took convincing for me to approach the idea of studying the teacher's perspective because I had been very interested in the student perspective for so long. But after my advisers lovingly poked and prodded at me, I embraced the idea and have never looked back. So, thank you Sandra and Mitch for starting me on this wonderful path long ago.

I surely would not be where I am today if I had not started my research project on Deb Borton, middle school choir teacher extraordinaire. She completely took me down the rabbit hole of empowering adolescent musicians; she taught me about Safe Place; and she embraced me as a colleague and a friend. She inspires my work every day and (even though I've tried to tell her) will have no idea of the magnitude of the impression that she has made on me and so many other people. I am a better music educator and human being for knowing her; the world is a much better place with her in it. Thank you, Deb.

The fourth person who has been key in the creation of this book is my editor at Oxford Press, Norm Hirschy. It was his vision to take the ideas from my dissertation and put them into a book to share with the world. He has been endlessly patient with me throughout this process—through changing university positions and moving across the country, through the arrival of both of my children—and has been nothing but 100 percent supportive and encouraging. His feedback is elegant and insightful; he is so good at helping me to see the forest for the trees. Norm, you have strengthened my voice as a music educator and I cannot thank you enough for believing in my work.

This project would not have been possible without the influence of the hundreds of adolescents with whom I've worked over the years. I am incredibly grateful to be a music educator and to work with so many remarkable students—both in my past and in my present. Thank you to all of the *amazing* middle school music teachers who shared their stories and love of teaching middle school students with me during this project: Michelle Barrientes, Bethany Cann, Robyn Chair (pseudonym), Jay Champion, James Cumings, Matthew Dethrow, Jason Freeland, Seth Gardner, Sean Grier, David Hirschorn, Mike Lehman, Marsha Miller (pseudonym), Andrew Nickles, Gretchen Pearson, Kate Tyler (pseudonym), and Tavia Zerman. I feel very fortunate to have crossed paths with you and am honored to share a bit of you with the music education profession.

I am especially thankful to Eve Harwood, who traded many hours of editing my proposal draft chapters for breakfast at Panera—you are one in a million. Thank you also to Janet Barrett and Louis Bergonzi, who have encouraged me and stretched my thinking with regard to Safe Place, diversity, and empowerment of adolescent musicians. I am so lucky to benefit from your guidance, your "push" to better understand what I am passionate about, and your incredible brains. Thank you to Eva Telzer and Reed W. Larson for your conversation, as well as your important insight and research on adolescents. Thank you to my students Katie Bruton, Meghan Jain, Megan Warren, and Syrus White for allowing me to share a bit of your personal insight. Thank you to Stacey Gross for all of your efforts to make this world a better place.

I have many supportive friends and colleagues who have helped me along this pathway. Thank you, especially, to Tami Draves and Mary Ann Schmedlen, who have asked repeatedly about this book project and always seem to supply the perfect encouraging words at the perfect time. I am also very appreciative of the great support that I have received from Christine Benway, Amy Davis, Kirstin Dougan, Doreen Earle, Lisa Koops, Adam

Kruse, Jeff Magee, Laurel Miller, Jeananne Nichols, Elizabeth Cassidy Parker, Heather Spitzley, Cynthia Taggart, and Sheri Tulloch.

Special thanks to my mom, Marsha Cosgrove, as well as my sister, Kate Cosgrove, for their continued love and support during the completion of this project. In addition, I am grateful for the love from Chris Tyler, Juniper Tyler, Patrick and Patricia Cosgrove, and the entire Sweet family (Deb and Tony, Abbey, Tiny and Erin, Sophia, Ava, and Vivian). A special note to my grandmother, Lillian Miller, who passed away while this book was still in progress at 100-1/2 years old: thank you for your unwavering love, support, and encouragement; you make me a better person.

To Luke and Evelyn, the greatest little people on the planet, I thank you for providing me with unlimited love and encouragement through your giggles, snuggles, spontaneous dance breaks, and silliness; and for allowing me breaks in my professional life to just be Momma. I love you madly and look forward to our time together when you are adolescents—it is going to be so much fun! And lastly, and most important, I am humbled by the unwavering love and support from my husband, Jason. I am not sure how I could have completed this book without you by my side and I am forever grateful for all of the kind and encouraging words, the hugs, and the Keurig coffeemaker that I have used a zillion times while writing late in the wee hours of the night or early in the wee hours of the morning. You have been so unselfish in giving me the time and space necessary for this project to come to fruition, always with a supportive or encouraging word. I love you and thank you for *everything*.

CHAPTER 1

The Adolescent Musician

BRIDGET: What do you enjoy about middle school students?

KATE (GENERAL MUSIC): Their sense of humor. *(She has a huge grin on her face as she speaks.)* I love that they wear their heart on their sleeves. And that they are just so ridiculously honest sometimes. I love that they can be a different person from one day to the next and when they appreciate something, they really appreciate it. And when they don't like something, they tell you! And they ask very frank questions that sometimes are difficult to answer, but they appreciate my honesty right back. So, in some ways, it's a little selfish of me because I get so much back from them, too. You know, I learn things from them and I get so much love from them, that it just comes full-circle and makes the whole thing worthwhile on a whole other level for me.

DEB (CHOIR): I got a chance to spend 24 hours with a whippet! Honest to God they don't even qualify as a dog—he's like a cat in a dog body! One of the funniest darn dogs! Their whole head is this wide! *(Deb holds up her thumb and pointer finger, just inches apart from each other.)* And his tail was like a possum! *(grimacing)* Ugh! Ryker the whippet. *(laughs)* See, I'll tell the kids about Ryker the whippet. I think that's a dog I can appreciate because that's like a middle-schooler. I mean this anomaly, this physical anomaly of boobs and hair and impulse and childhood and the whole middle school child just delights me. And they still love you. They are still young enough to be able to love you openly, which I think is quite delightful.

If you described the young adolescent music student, what words would you choose? Emotional? Quirky? Irrational? Witty? Awkward? Funny? Hormonal? Smelly? A whippet? All of the above and more? When working with young adolescents, music teachers may encounter a range of possible characteristics on any given day with any given student. The following remark by Tim Gerber in his article "Nurturing the Young Adolescent: High Stakes for the School and Social Environment" accurately describes adolescents:

> Young adolescents can switch from sweet to sullen in seconds. They can be friendly one day and distant the next. They can go from being naïve nerds to party animals in the same week. They seek attention for being weird or unique, but then quickly conform to bathe in the security of peer approval. They wallow in egocentric excess—only to snap suddenly out of it. (Gerber 1994, 7)

Unfortunately, research and writings have complicated understandings of adolescents (and adolescence) by focusing on the age group with a deficit viewpoint, highlighting instances of unpredictability, risk-taking, or negative decision-making rather than on instances of ability, loyalty, and humor. In his book *Adolescence*, Ian McMahan illustrates this point:

> I dropped by a large bookstore and browsed in the Parenting department. The books were arranged by age. On the first shelves, I noticed such titles as *The Magic Years, How to Raise a Happy Baby,* and *Kids Are Worth It.* The covers featured cute, smiling babies and attractive, smiling parents. Then I moved a few feet to the right, to the Adolescence section. Some of the titles caught my eye: *The Roller Coaster Years, How to Keep Your Teenager Out of Trouble, How to Stop the Battle with Your Teenager, How to Keep Your Teenager from Driving You Crazy, Yes, Your Teen Is Crazy!* Clearly, the idea that adolescence has to be a time of "storm and stress" is alive and well and living at Barnes & Noble! (McMahan 2008, 156)

Along the same lines, in *Teaching General Music in Grades 4–8,* music education professor Thomas Regelski discourages broad, negative assumptions about adolescence: " 'Storm and stress' is not a universal experience of early adolescence. Some individuals are (or seem to be) well adjusted" (Regelski 2004, 35).

I believe that early adolescence is a time of delightful and rocky individual transition for everyone regardless of intelligence, ability, or popularity level. I also believe that as music educators we are in prime positions to provide safe places and experiences for middle school students to learn about music *and* themselves, free from judgment. When adolescent music students sense less scrutiny from others and feel accepted for who they are, students experience feelings of empowerment and are more willing to put themselves out there with regard to their music and thinking.

My experience as an adolescent student was not overtly negative, but also not great. What about yours? I encourage you to recall and reflect on your own adolescent experiences to retain a personal perspective on the age group. As a result, you will be better equipped to recognize and reconcile various characteristics of your adolescent music students. When contemplating your own experiences, also recall the role that music played. In my own adolescent reality, choir class kept me going throughout any minor or major turmoil; similarly, for many of our students, music is an escape, an adventure, a home away from home, and a bright spot in their days.

Focus of this first chapter is on key characteristics that should be considered by music educators working with adolescents, regardless of area of musical concentration. The following discussions are based on the collected wisdom of individual teachers and findings of scholarly research.

CHARACTERISTICS TO CONSIDER

Puberty refers to the onset of adult reproductive capacity. As a milestone in human development, puberty is quite dramatic, involving a rapid transformation of anatomy, physiology and behavior. Other than pregnancy, it is probably the most abrupt and encompassing developmental transition that human beings undergo between birth and death. (Ellison and Reiches 2012, 81)

There is no precise span of years to define "adolescence," but teachers and researchers tend to agree that this developmental period extends across middle school and high school, perhaps into the early twenties. As a choral teacher, I have worked with students in the beginning stages of voice change (signifying the start of puberty, often considered the official start of adolescence) in upper elementary school as well as in early high school. Therefore, discussion of the adolescent student throughout this book is not strictly limited to students in grades six through eight. And, although generalizations may be made about adolescent characteristics and behaviors, music educators must consider each student on an individual basis.

As mentioned earlier, although the word "adolescence" does conjure negative feelings and/or images for some people, this is not the case for everyone. While writing this book, I met with Eva Telzer, a developmental psychologist at the University of Illinois. Over coffee we discussed the dominant perception that adolescence is believed to be a dark time of depression and horribleness for developing teens. This widespread bias has, in turn, influenced research on adolescents (and adolescence) in that much focus is maintained on negative aspects of this developmental period rather than positive aspects. Many people do have positive recollections of adolescence, especially those involved with music. Because of this, music teachers are encouraged to remember throughout this chapter (and book) that adolescence is a time when music students are primed to be influenced and to grow and contribute in all kinds of positive and exciting ways.

Physical Nuances

At the onset of puberty, secondary sex characteristics begin to emerge. In girls there is the rounding out of hips, breast development, appearance of pubic hair, menstruation, and change of voice. In boys, there is a broadening of chest, appearance of pubic hair, facial hair, and change of voice. It is also during this time that middle school students start to take precautions about body odor and begin to (optimistically) use deodorant and (unfortunately) much too much cologne or body spray.

Poor posture is often an issue with adolescents as a result of self-conscious feelings about personal appearance and rate of growth. In addition, people commonly react to adolescents more on the basis of size than age. Physically small adolescents may be viewed as immature or as less-skilled musicians, even if these students have high intellectual abilities. On the other hand, adolescents who are physically large for their age, even though they are emotionally and intellectually immature, are expected to act grown-up and to do or know more than what they are capable of.

The range of possibilities for adolescent physiological development is very wide, and the bottom line is that nothing is predictable. Picture a group of seventh grade boys. What do you see? A realistic vision would be one long, lanky student who towers over the rest, standing next to a tiny student who is easily mistaken for a fourth-grader, standing next to a stocky baby-faced student who is standing next to the stereotypical quarterback on the high school football team. Arms so long that students can practically scratch the backs of their knees without bending over. Incredibly long feet. Noses and ears and mouths too big for faces. Similar contrasting descriptions could also easily be conjured for a group of adolescent girls. Each student will grow at a different rate and, as developmental psychologist Ian McMahan explains, some even with body parts growing at different rates.

The growth spurt in adolescence does not go smoothly and evenly. Different parts of the body change at different times and at different rates. Children who have recently entered their growth spurt sometimes have the feeling their hands and feet aren't where they're supposed to be. The reason is that hands and feet, along with the head, are the first parts of the body to start growing faster at puberty. The arms and legs follow soon after. Growth in the trunk and shoulders comes still later. This asynchronicity is responsible for the "gawky," "gangly," or "leggy" look that makes so many early adolescents self-conscious about their appearance. (McMahan 2008, 72)

In addition, adolescents are clumsy, poorly coordinated, and often trip over themselves purely because they no longer know how long their feet actually are. Linda Perlstein beautifully describes this sporadic, erratic growth in *Not Much Just Chillin'*:

It happens at different times for everyone, which is why there are kids in sixth grade who look eight and kids who look eighteen. These physical changes are the greatest they've experienced since they were babies. This mysterious force that visits preteen boy's bodies, which causes blond hair to darken and easy grace to disappear in a tangle of limbs and skin to pock with pimples, is objectively something wonderful—growth! change! maturity!—but it infuses them with a profound, unidentifiable sense of loss, as they start to see their childhoods fall. They're not so cute anymore, and they know it. Their smells outpace their awareness of them, feet and armpits and breath, such that sixth-grade teachers wonder if they can tell their first-period classes to brush their teeth, or should they have the nurse do it? Eventually muscles will form, visible through fore-arms when fingers are flexed, but for now the bones come alone, and arms and legs grow faster than the brain's ability to track them. A boy hits himself on corners of doorways, bangs his funny bone. So many times, as he races to get his gym clothes off to catch the bus home, Jimmy gets his head stuck in his shirt, the pants in the shoes, so he's starting to wear his gym clothes home. Entering puberty, a child grows so fast (three inches a year, on average, for boys) and so unevenly that inactivity is actually painful. He squirms after sitting still for fourteen minutes, which makes eighty-minute classes excruciating. Why do the teachers make you sit up straight? They think you can learn only if your body is propped a certain way? (Perlstein 2003, 61–62)

Sporadic physical growth presents potential challenges for our adolescent musicians as they struggle to retain control of gross and fine motor skills. With longer fingers and arms, students may have difficulty negotiating their instruments in our music classes; with longer legs, activities such as dancing, movement, or marching can be quite challenging. All of this should give you a whole new respect for well-synchronized middle school marching bands. And speaking of marching bands:

> MARSHA (BAND): I had this one trumpet player who was marching with his trumpet and, while playing [the music] memorized, bent down at the same time, picked up a rock, and threw it at another kid. And I was just like, "What are you doing?!" And I just wanted to be so mad at him because he threw a rock at somebody else—but at the same time I was like, "That was so impressive!" *(chuckles)* He was able to do that ... I couldn't believe that the kid had enough coordination to do this!

In the article "Physical, Motor, and Fitness Development in Children and Adolescents," authors Leonard D. Zaichkowsky and Gerald A. Larson discuss the development of gross and fine motor skills of children and adolescents. They organized their discussion by age grouping: early childhood, childhood (6–9 years), late childhood (10–12 years), and adolescence (12–18 years). Because adolescents will experience puberty at different rates, our students will likely embody a combination of characteristics of both late childhood (10–12 years) and adolescence (12–18 years) in our music classes.

During late childhood (10–12 years), children are especially full of energy and experience their greatest changes in motor skills. In addition:

> During this period children move from *fundamental*, transitional motor skills to the development of *specific* skills, and more fine-motor skills. Major pubertal changes occur; girls often experience an early growth spurt and surpass boys in physical and motor development until the later adolescent growth spurt of boys occurs. (Zaichkowsky and Larson 1995, 63; emphasis in original)

Consider students you know around this age. Can you think of specific students who have largely mastered gross motor skills (such as playing a percussion instrument on the beat or singing a processional while walking onto risers) but struggle with tasks that require more fine motor skills (such as playing a cross-hand arpeggio on an Orff instrument, articulating a scale on the piano, or flawlessly demonstrating an intricate physical movement sequence)? Does sex and/or gender play a role in student success of some tasks over others?

All of your students will increase mastery of both gross and fine motor skills to some degree during their time in your music classes, but it will take some adolescents longer than others. Therefore, what are the implications of this "skill transition time" for us as music teachers? First and foremost, we must remain patient. There is no sense in being frustrated about something that is completely out of everyone's control. What *is* within control is careful and thoughtful planning of lessons that allow students to engage with music and feel successful on some level, regardless of their developmental stage. In addition, lessons and activities need to be sequenced in such a way that students build and develop skills both within a single class period as well as over several class periods.

As adolescents enter into seventh and eighth grades, characteristics described by Zaichkowsky and Larson for the stage of adolescence (12–18 years) will emerge, beginning with an early growth spurt that "is so rapid that motor abilities lag behind" (1995, 64). This period of development coincides with great motor awkwardness, as addressed earlier. However, according to Zaichkowsky and Larson, alongside the significant increases in awkwardness, physical strength, and size during adolescence, students will also begin to experience a refinement of motor skills that leads to a desire for specialization in activities. "The specialization stage of motor development continues through adulthood. It is characterized by the individual's desire to participate in a limited number of activities and represents a combination of all preceding stages" (ibid.). Therefore, at this peak time of great physical awkwardness and unpredictability, students start to make key choices about their musical involvement—largely based on current perceptions of their abilities at musical tasks. Again, *at a time when they are the most awkward*, students make big choices about their future involvement in music. It is a dangerous intersection for us as music teachers and we must proceed wisely to help our students feel successful and understand that physical skills will catch up to cognitive learning in due time, meanwhile keeping our music programs meaningful and relevant for adolescent musicians.

During my years teaching middle school choir, adolescent male and female voice change was commonly a fork in the road for students making decisions about future involvement with singing, both within my choral program and beyond middle school. But before I continue with this example, I would like to briefly explain what happens during voice change. The most simplistic of explanations is that voice change is a growth spurt of the larynx. When adolescent body parts are growing sporadically, the larynx also grows in size. The larynx is the walnut-sized house for the vocal folds located in the middle of one's neck as part of the trachea (also known as the windpipe). In males, the larynx grows more posteriorly/anteriorly (front to back) resulting in the protrusion of the Adam's apple in the neck for most young men. The female larynx tends to grow more in height or round out a bit, which is why females tend to not have an Adam's apple after they pass through puberty.

In addition to the overall larynx enlarging, everything within the larynx also grows, including cartilage, muscles, and the vocal folds. Female vocal folds elongate approximately 3 to 4 millimeters, resulting in a singing range extension downward one-third of an octave and up 3 to 4 pitches when all is settled; male vocal folds elongate approximately 1 centimeter, resulting in a downward-range extension of one octave and upwards 6 to 7 pitches. So all of the components of the larynx continue to operate as normal, but because muscles that control cartilage, which in turn controls the vocal folds, are all growing at sporadic rates, the vocal folds cannot close properly (or all the way) until this entire growth spurt is complete. As a result, both male and female singers experience a lack of phonation on certain pitches or large "holes" in the singing range, cracking and fuzzy voices, excessive breathiness (because vocal folds are not closed all the way and air is escaping through the space between them), a thin or colorless vocal tone, and great unpredictability during vocal production.[1]

I now turn back to the example introduced above. Because voice change can be so personal and unpredictable, it can largely influence adolescents to stop singing. Therefore, in my choir classes I employed key tactics to keep students singing and feeling normal during voice change. First, I made a formal presentation about what physiologically happens during voice change, and I did this every year with every choir. So if I had an eighth-grade student for all three years of middle school, that student took part in my official presentation about voice change three times. This is very important, because each subsequent time, the student was in a new phase of voice change and interested in different aspects of my presentation. Beyond the formal presentation, acknowledgment of voice change was woven into the fabric of our choral classroom and a common topic of conversation. I hung posters of the respiratory system and digestive system around the room and referenced them often; we watched videos of laryngoscopes and people singing, as well as videos of middle school students singing at different stages of voice change; students assisted in their own voice testing at least four times per year; students constantly sang different voice parts in the music so that no one was permanently associated with a particular voice part (on this song you are singing alto vs. you are an alto); students assisted me in rearranging their own vocal lines according to the accessible notes; and we celebrated the little and big successes of individuals ("I can sing down to an F below middle C now!"), as well as the larger group ("That is the fastest that you have ever tuned that chord! Bravo to you!").

Praising students for what they can do!

All of these conversations and efforts were important because I wanted my students to feel empowered by understanding what was happening with their voices, as well as realizing that voice change was not a big mystery. Too many students visualize their voice as the glowing orb that was Ariel's voice in *The Little Mermaid* and call it good. But from all of these efforts in my class, can you guess what happened? Students, overall, were okay with dealing with vocal challenges because we just put it out there: *everyone* will have their own experience with voice change, so let's just work together and embrace it. As a result, students kept singing, even if they could only sing two notes in tune for several weeks at a time. Mentally and emotionally they were supported, and so they went for it in most situations. Then, when students physiologically started to regain control of their voices—maybe this was during their time with me or perhaps after they had moved on to the high school choir—their drive and knowledge was already in forward motion and everything just fell beautifully into place.

Therefore, to bring it all together, I have found it to be imperative that adolescent students stay mentally and emotionally upbeat about any sort of physiological development they are experiencing, armed with an understanding of what is happening and knowing that the strife will not last forever. With understanding and a sense of power over their body's transitional processes (as a result of their understanding), when it came time for my students to specialize in a craft through the scheduling of their classes, there was a far greater chance that music was a contender for their attention. As you consider your own students, ask yourself: In what ways can you neutralize the awkwardness of adolescent physical development in your music classes and embolden adolescents to keep learning music until motor skill development settles?

Adolescent Emotion

As a middle school choir teacher, I was fortunate to work with students for multiple years as they moved through sixth, seventh, and eighth grades. One of my favorite aspects of our time together was witnessing their transitions of cognitive and emotional development from grade to grade. There are vast differences between the three age groups of middle school, regardless of where one works or teaches. Sixth graders come from elementary school and are characteristically young and energetic; they are willing to try most anything and are fiercely loyal once you get them on your side. The seventh grade year is a time of transition from being a spritely sixth grader to a more reserved eighth grader. Seventh graders are fearless and excitable; they can be incredibly mature one moment and ridiculously goofy the next. Musically, they are either greatly in control of the task at hand or all over the board. Eighth grade students are more reserved when it comes to tasks that might embarrass them—such as a simple movement exercise—and can be challenging to motivate if the task has no real-world connection to their existence. However, eighth graders are physically able to perform musical tasks on a different level from sixth or seventh graders, as they start to regain control of their changing body.

Because our adolescent music students are straddling both their child and adult selves, we must value both worlds. In addition, it is imperative to respect the space that students are in from moment to moment and utilize effective strategies for working with students depending on where *they* are from moment to moment. If your students are in a "silly kid" space, initially approaching them with silly-kid-energy tasks and expectations will be much more effective than approaching them in this moment with tasks and expectations requiring a more mature mind frame. You can transition them from one space to another during rehearsal or class, but must begin with the energy that *they* bring to the classroom rather than your teaching agenda for the day.

In addition to acknowledging the emotional fluctuation of our students, it is also important for us to be aware that adolescents often misplace emotions, especially negative ones. Adolescents can struggle in relationships with parents, siblings, and peers and are often unsure of how to articulate what they are feeling. Most commonly, adolescent emotions are either expressed through tears or an emotional explosion, usually taken out on someone who has nothing to do with the situation at hand. As music teachers, our work with students for three or four consecutive years provides us with wonderful opportunities to build close, trusting relationships with individual students. However, because of the closeness of our relationships, students often look to us (consciously or unconsciously) as safe places and outlets for emotional release. This is not to say that students have a right to vent all frustrations in our direction; they do not. However, we must recognize the difference between types of misbehavior or insubordination and struggles within a personal crisis. A story from my own experience:

Julie arrived to class as she did every day, but did not get her music folder on her way to her seat. Following warm-ups, we launched into our first piece of the rehearsal and I noticed that Julie did not have her music. "Julie, please get your folder so that you are looking on your own music and not that of your neighbor." Julie *exploded*. "I HATE this class!" *(jumping up from her chair)* "I am dropping this class IMMEDIATELY and NEVER coming back! I HATE it!"

What would your immediate reaction have been? Anger in response? Sending her to the principal's office? Would you remember that other students are watching your reaction? How would you treat the other students in the music class after such an incident? How do you show authority and "save face" in this situation? As a beginning teacher, I would have been very angry and probably sent her to the in-school suspension room to fill out a disciplinary packet for her outburst. However, when this particular situation happened I was (fortunately) experienced enough to recognize that this explosion had nothing at all to do with me. In reality, Julie's brother had attempted suicide the previous evening and she was severely struggling with the situation and how to handle all of her emotions.

Adolescent struggles to process emotions, both great and small, are often complicated by self-imposed feelings of loneliness and isolation. The belief that one's own thoughts, feelings, and experiences are unique is referred to as a "personal fable," an idea published by David Elkind in his 1967 article "Egocentrism in Adolescence" and summarized here by Ian McMahan:

> Adolescents do confront so many feelings, situations, and challenges that are absolutely new to them. The first time you fall in love, the first time a friend drops you, the first time you see your parents as ordinary and fallible, is unique to you. It never happened to you before. It is just a short step from the realization, "*I* never felt like this before," to the conclusion, "*No one* ever felt like this before." If someone then pats your shoulder and says, "I know how you feel," the only possible response is an emphatic, "No, you don't. You *can't!*" (McMahan, 2009, 114; emphasis in original)

Acknowledging student emotion and not immediately dismissing it as extreme—even though it may feel that way to us as an adult—is important, especially when working with adolescent music students. Music, by its very nature, can be emotional and trigger unexpected emotional responses that may or may not be related to the task at hand. Somehow student emotions need to be validated or acknowledged, even with something as simple as, "I am sorry that you are feeling so upset by. . . ." That way, adolescents feel heard and acknowledged while we, as the teacher, are not supporting or berating the emotion at hand. In chapter 2, the idea of music teacher as counselor will be briefly discussed; in chapter 4 the idea of misbehavior stemming from problems outside the music classroom will be discussed. Both could be considered extensions of this conversation here.

Brain Development

Brain development is a popular topic in conversations on adolescent development. However, as I will discuss in this section, the phrase "development of the adolescent brain" is too commonly used as a broad, sweeping explanation to justify adolescent behaviors and choices, especially those that are different or less desirable than the social norm. Scientists and researchers acknowledge that physiological changes do occur in the adolescent brain, but in ways that stretch beyond those that are conventionally acknowledged by society.

In the *Handbook of Adolescent Psychology*, cognitive development professor Deanna Kuhn composed a chapter titled "Adolescent Thinking" in which she addressed a variety of topics that revolve around adolescent brain development. Three of these discussions particularly pertain to our dialogue here. The first is biological. Via Kuhn's words, let us gain a basic understanding of two kinds of change that take place in the prefrontal cortex of the brain during adolescence:

> Modern longitudinal neuroimaging research reports two kinds of change, one in the so-called gray matter, which undergoes a wave of overproduction (paralleling one occurring in the early years) at puberty, followed by a reduction, or "pruning," of those neuronal connections that do not continue to be used. A second change, in so-called white matter, is enhanced myelination, that is, increased insulation of established neuronal connections, improving their efficiency. By the end of adolescence, then, this evidence suggests, teens have fewer, more selective, but stronger, more effective neuronal connections than they did as children. (Kuhn 2009, 153)

So in relation to our work as music teachers, it is helpful to remember that as adolescents begin to devote more time, or even specialize, in specific activities—whether they be music, athletics, debate, comic books, or student government—the brain responds accordingly to lock in and protect knowledge learned and skills gained. Oppositely, the above is exactly as it sounds: if you don't use it, you lose it.

Secondly in her chapter, Kuhn expressed concern that reports on adolescent brain development have "attracted the interest and imagination of the media" (ibid., 153). As a result, the media have drawn a variety of conclusions about adolescent brain development to provide an explanation for all adolescent behaviors and choices (similar to the Mozart Effect fiasco of the 1990s). Kuhn cited the book *The Primal Teen: What the New Discoveries about the Teenage Brain Tells Us about Our Kids*, written by Barbara Strauch

(2003), to be a fine example of a misleading publication about adolescent brain development.

> Strauch points to incomplete brain development as an explanation for just about everything about adolescents that adults have found perplexing, from sleep patterns to risk taking and mood swings. In the cognitive realm, Strauch quotes approvingly a middle-school teacher's comment that it is good to know that "if you have an adolescent in a seventh-grade science class and he or she is having difficulty with abstract concepts, it may . . . have to do with brain development and developmental readiness." Such an inference warrants concern because it absolves less-than-optimal instructions as a possible contributor, among other reasons. (ibid., 154)

This is not to say that Kuhn does not acknowledge that the brain develops during adolescence, but rather she encourages readers to consider that adolescent brain development alone does not guide all adolescent behaviors. Rather—which brings us to the third topic that I wish to highlight from Kuhn's chapter—student experiences can be powerful enough to, themselves, guide brain development. A widely accepted conclusion among developmental neuropsychologists (Huttenlocher 2002; Nelson, Thomas, and de Hann 2006; Thomas and Johnson 2008) is that "development of the brain is dependent on experience. In other words, there cannot exist a simple, unidirectional, causal relation between brain developments and outcomes at a behavioral or psychological level" (Kuhn 2009, 154).

Kuhn is one of many scientists promoting broader considerations of the adolescent brain. Another is Tomás Paus, a professor of population neuroscience. Paus focused his chapter, "Brain Development" (also published in the *Handbook on Adolescent Psychology*), on the relationship between genes and environment in shaping brain development. Paus discussed mounting scientific evidence that indicates brain function and development to not be as simplistic as "genes influencing the brain directly and, in turn, the individual's behavior" (Paus 2009, 110). In other words, brain development is not a one-way street from childhood to adulthood, guided only by genetic factors. Rather, environmental experiences themselves may have a cumulative effect on developmental changes in brain structure.

> Given the role of experience in shaping the brain, it might also be that high demands on cognitive control faced, for example, by young adolescents assuming adult roles due to family circumstances may facilitate structural maturation of their prefrontal cortex. This scenario, if proven correct, will move us away

from the "passive" view of brain development into one that emphasizes an active role of the individual and his/her environment in modulating the "biological" (e.g., hormonal) developmental processes. (ibid., 110)

Along with this, recent brain research has also shown that attempts at new challenges and learning from one's mistakes can be quite beneficial to adolescent brain development and function. The following comes from the book *The Owner's Manual for Driving Your Adolescent Brain*:

> Making mistakes occurs frequently when learning more complicated skills that require multiple parts of the brain. This is good! Newer research is showing that making mistakes actually enhances the function of the prefrontal cortex and corpus callosum. When you have to struggle, think, figure out what to do next, fail, and try again, you are giving these parts a good workout and strengthening the neural pathways necessary to get the job done right. Don't wait until you have the right answer or just do what is easy. It's okay to make mistakes—they will make you stronger, if you use them as an opportunity to learn! (Deak and Deak 2013, 57)

The bottom line is that adolescent brain development is complicated—very, very complicated—and not a viable explanation for all adolescent behavior and choices, especially as research has shown the brain to be greatly influenced by experiences and environment. With regard to the music classroom, there are three big take-aways from the aforementioned brain research. One: adolescents should have opportunities to strengthen neural pathways by using multiple parts of their brain to think about music critically, experiment with trial and error, break musical ideas apart and put them back together again, and learn from mistakes. In addition, tasks should be customized to individual students or groupings of students, but varied and challenging enough to promote student learning and encourage future involvement with music.

Two: the music class environment, itself, plays a role in adolescent brain development. Although class environment is addressed in greater detail in chapters three and four, for now consider how the atmosphere fostered in your own music classroom potentially influences and advances the brain development of your students, which can in turn influence adolescent behavior and future participation in music.

Three: as musical ideas and concepts are introduced to our adolescent students, remember that the adolescent brain protects specific established neuronal connections that are accessed often and perceived as valuable. On the flipside, connections made but rarely accessed will most likely be pruned away by the brain to make room for more important neuronal connections. Again, if you don't use it, you lose it. Too often in music education, students are provided lists of terms to memorize and regurgitate, but they never truly understand how the term is used in practice or why (or how) it makes music more special. Musical ideas, terms, and concepts must be revisited often and in varied and meaningful ways for adolescent brains to solidify them for the long-term. Ultimately, deeper explorations of fewer musical topics will "stick" with adolescents because they will understand the significance of what they are learning much more than brief encounters with many topics in a shallow manner.

Cognition

It is important to acknowledge the array of learning styles of your students when working with adolescents. In the book *Boys and Girls Learn Differently: A Guide for Teachers and Parents,* authors Michael Gurian and Kathy Stevens address areas of learning-style difference between males and females, each supported by brain-based research. Below, I share excerpts from this discussion and contribute my own music education twist following each excerpt. However, even though Gurian and Stevens parse specific differences between genders, continue to keep in mind that every adolescent thinks and processes information uniquely, so there are exceptions to all of the following in each of our music classes, regardless of gender. Consideration of these ideas will help to inform our music teaching practice and reinforce the importance of a multifaceted approach in order to "catch" all adolescent music students in some way.

Abstract and Concrete Reasoning

Boys tend to be better than girls at not seeing or touching the thing and yet still being able to calculate it. For example, when mathematics is taught on a blackboard, boys often do better at it than girls. Females prefer when a concept is taught using manipulatives and objects—that is, taken off the blackboard, out of the abstract world of signs and signifiers, and put into the concrete world. (Gurian and Stevens 2011, 45)

- A music class example: Teaching a concept such as chord structure on staff paper will help many students gain an understanding of chord structure, but not all students. For those who need a more concrete approach, chord structure could also be taught (and reinforced) by handing out handbell chimes to students and rearranging individuals to form various "human chords" to learn the concept in a more kinesthetic fashion. Another music class example: teaching the concept of tension and resolution. In addition to listening to musical examples and discussing the use of text or poetry in a song (perhaps also comparing the use of music *with* the use of text), students can experience tension and resolution more concretely through movement. For example, tension can be experienced through "bound flow" exercises by pushing on a wall (real or imagined) with all one's strength; juxtapose this with "free flow" exercises by allowing students to individually mimick swimming movements in place or around the room. Moving immediately from one to the other allows adolescents to experience the concept of tension and resolution in a physical way–bound flow versus free flow–solidifying the concept more fully as well as kinesthetically demonstrating differences in intensity between tension and resolve intended by a composer or songwriter.

Use of Language

During the learning process, we often find girls using words *as they learn*, and boys often working silently. Girls also tend to prefer to have things conceptualized in usable, everyday language, replete with concrete details. Boys often find jargon and coded language more interesting. (ibid., 2011, 45–46; emphasis in original)

- In music class: Allowing students to talk through musical problems and arrive at solutions is important. Not everyone will desire to chat away with their neighbor, but never allowing students time to freely contemplate concepts out loud (e.g., poetry or text in music, word painting, compositional techniques, societal context surrounding a musical piece, reactions to a piece of music) may stifle some students' learning and creativity. In addition, the idea of pairing simplistic language with technical jargon works beautifully in music: *pianissimo* = soft. Allowing students to use the set of terminology with which they are most comfortable (perhaps even their own set of invented or adapted terms?) can increase their attention to such details in music class and perhaps help students to make more meaningful connections between music and their everyday lives.

Engaging Brains

Given how quickly the brain is growing during these years, variety is in itself quite useful for engaging boys' and girls' brains. (ibid., 249)

- In music class: Keep discussion and instructions clean, clear, and to the point. Provide instructions in multiple formats when possible, such as verbal explanation in addition to written instructions. Emphasize key points by rephrasing ideas in several ways to catch the different listeners in your music classes. As will be discussed further in chapter 4, adolescent attention spans are short and must be considered: limit lecture or instructions to around five minutes followed by 10 to 15 minutes of the students *doing* (such as listening, singing, playing, composing, improvising); repeat.

Movement

Girls do not generally need to move around as much while learning. Movement seems to help boys not only stimulate their brains but also manage and relieve impulsive behavior. Movement is also natural to boys in a closed space, possibly a result of their higher levels of spinal fluid moving between the brain and the body and higher metabolism, which creates fidgeting behavior. (ibid., 47)

- I am a firm believer that movement improves learning for *everyone*— even the smallest movements can have an important impact. There is absolutely no reason that movement cannot be naturally woven into any music class activity, especially if it is shown to benefit student learning. As mentioned earlier in this chapter, physical growth can be painful for adolescents; a little movement may provide students relief from growing pains for a short time, allowing them to focus better on the musical task at hand. In addition, movement allows for kinesthetic examples of musical ideas, contributing to greater abstract and concrete reasoning and understanding in the music classroom (as discussed above). In turn, additional understanding contributes to feelings of accomplishment in music classes, which can influence adolescents' depth of involvement with music.

In addition to acknowledging differences in students' learning styles, it is also worth noting that adolescents sharpen their ability to think abstractly and draw conclusions from given information during cognitive development. As an example, Marsha (band) shared a story about her habits of drawing conclusions during adolescence: "If the person next to me was playing really sharp, I thought that if I played really flat, it would make us in tune. I was the perfect middle schooler for drawing her own conclusions." Also during adolescence, contemplative skills are budding and the ability to interpret and understand symbolism increases, especially in music and song lyrics. In addition, adolescent use and understanding of humor is maturing and *they* are humorous, whether they realize it or not.

NAVIGATING IDENTITY

Adolescents are neither children nor adults, and they are caught in the middle of a variety of expectations from parents and other adult figures. For example, the role of a child is structured and clear because the child knows what they can and cannot do. Generally, children are expected to attend school and be respectful and kind to others. Expectations within households exist for children, such as completing their chores or helping with a younger brother or sister. The role of an adult is also structured and clear. Adults are expected to be responsible for themselves in addition to providing food and shelter for themselves and, perhaps, a family. Adults are expected to vote in elections and work to be well-adjusted members of society. However, because the role of the adolescent is not as clearly defined, the young person does not quite know where they may stand with regard to personal identity.

Adolescents want more independence as the desire grows to achieve adult status; they want to run their own lives and be less reliant on parental figures; they want to be validated by peers and adults they admire; they want to be their own person, yet not stick out too much. In our work as middle school music teachers, it is essential to acknowledge that our students want to be *treated* like adults and are striving for an adult identity. Therefore, we can hold our music students to very high standards and treat them as we would treat anyone else. However, we must also recognize that no matter how badly middle school students want to be adult-like, they are still partially in their child-selves. So while upholding music students to high standards, they also need ego strokes, structure, patience, accountability, and genuine caring.

Middle school students tend to be social creatures. They form social groups—often moving from single-sex groups to co-ed groups—and enjoy talking to one another and spending time together. It is not unusual to see our students move between circles during their middle school years as they start to figure out who they are socially, intellectually, emotionally, and sexually. Through participation in different groups, adolescents "try on" various personal identities to learn about what fits them best for the present day as well as for the longer term (which could be something completely different from their short-term identity). Here is some student perspective on social grouping from *Fires in the Middle School Bathroom*:

> Most of the time, it's just girls or just boys [who hang out together]—unless some are brave enough to break the group. One group of girls always bring a jump rope, and so some boys will get in that group and be jumping rope, trying to get in. Most of the groups have a major thing they like to talk about. There's one group that likes to go to the library. Boys that like football a lot. Others that like to hang out and beat up on kids. There are girls that just like to hang out and talk. (Jason, grade 7.) (Cushman and Rogers 2008, 21)

> There's a girl popular group and a boy popular group, and a Spanish girl popular group and a Spanish boy popular group. Then there's the normal people and the geeks, and the people who don't stay with anything, people who skateboard. And the groups of people who are really athletic—mostly the popular boys—and the girls who act like they're hanging out with them. (Genesis, grade 7.) (ibid., 21)

In 1965, Glenn Myers Blair and R. Stewart Jones authored *Psychology of Adolescence for Teachers* and wrote about three human personality needs that are of great importance to an adolescent: the need for status, independence, and achievement. Although Blair and Jones's work was published many years ago, their viewpoints remain incredibly relevant today. "Status in the peer group is probably more important to many adolescents than status in the eyes of their parents or teachers; yet recognition from both of these sources is cherished by adolescents" (Blair and Jones 1965, 8). As a result, adolescents often act unpredictably as they consider who they are and who they want to be, all while in the midst of constantly changing peer relationships and worrying about others' opinions—that neverending, relentless scrutiny from an imaginary audience.

Complicating matters, adolescent music students develop an acute awareness of conformity versus nonconformity among peers in their school setting during times of identity formation. As the "peer group provides stability (or consistency) and provides the opportunity to practice social relationships and roles" (Regelski 2004, 34), it can also positively and/or negatively influence involvement in school music programs and musician identity development, depending upon how music classes are deemed by the desired peer group. For my master's thesis I spoke with groups of current and former middle school choral students about reasons why they did or did not continue participation in choir when it was no longer a school requirement. And although the following finding cannot be generalized to all teaching settings, peers are clearly an influential factor on some adolescents' participation in music:

> Peers seemed to be more influential to former choir students than to current choir students. The current choir students indicated that it was nice having friends in choir, but friends or peers were not the main factor for their returning to choir class. The former choir students, however, indicated that peers were quite important and where their friends went, they would go. Therefore, it could be concluded from the results of this study that friends and peers are a main factor in some students' decisions of whether to remain in choir. The students who remained in choir must have been influenced by factors that are more compelling than peers. In addition, it is a possibility that these students' friends remained in choir, so these current choir students remained in choir. (Sweet, 2003, 141)

To summarize: in music classes, adolescents navigate musical and social expectations put forth by their peers, in addition to navigating new musical experiences and expectations put forth by the music teacher, all while negotiating child vs. adult roles and responsibilities. These factors also mix with ideas and opinions about music (and music's role in one's life) that our students embody from their home environments and personal cultures, largely influenced by family members. Consequently, student motivation to participate in music class, as well as reaction to various musical experiences, is truly influenced by a wide variety of factors.

Therefore, the more connections that we make among musical ideas, our students' everyday lives, and identity exploration will not only assist adolescents in learning more about themselves through our music classes but also provide deeper and more meaningful connections to our subject matter. The big implication here is that we cannot assume that students will come to music class ready to learn everything we have to offer because: 1) many are already preoccupied with other, seemingly more pressing adolescent matters; 2) many cannot see the big picture of the importance of music education in their developing identities or lives.

There is a great scene in the beginning of the 2007 movie, *Superbad*, (a raunchy teen/coming-of-age comedy written by Seth Rogan and Evan Goldberg; not for the faint of heart or easily offended) in which the character Seth (played by Jonah Hill) is talking to his home economics teacher. At the beginning of this particular scene, he is too preoccupied by discussions of drinking, sex, and maintaining a "cool" identity with his friends to care much about making the tiramisu that has been assigned by the teacher. He ends up trying to explain to her that he is a senior in high school and, in the grand scheme of his life (as he sees it), he will never make tiramisu again; he sees no point in the assignment (Apatow & Mottola, 2007).

I find this particular scene to be a pretty accurate depiction of our work as music teachers of adolescents: we come to class hoping our students inherently want to search for meaning in what we teach, but realistically we have to provide clear and blunt answers to the "So what?" question. We have to help them get invested. We have to show them why they should care about what we are teaching, as well as how music will assist them on their journeys of self-discovery and identity formation. We do this by providing means for meaningful connections between what we teach and their own personal lives.

As you ponder ways to establish such connections in your music classrooms, a starting point might be something along the lines of what I did with my own middle school choral students. For the "Identity Music Project" students shared music that was poignant to them thus far in their life. Students were invited to select five one-minute snippets of influential songs and provide a little background on them prior to sharing each one with the class. This project was never a requirement, but strongly encouraged for those interested. Each day I would ask if someone had a project to share and, inevitably, one or two people would have a five-piece collection of one-minute snippets of songs to share. (In chapter two I will discuss a similar task that you can use to learn more about yourself as a music educator.)

Through this project, my music students learned a great deal about themselves as well as each other. Students shared specific sections of songs for a wide variety of reasons. I witnessed students taking a stand against the social structure of schools and society through their carefully selected song snippets. I learned a great deal about students' relationships with their parents–some heartwarming and some concerning. I watched my entire class shed tears and bond, moved by stories of brave loved ones who had died from cancer and loved a particular song or by songs honoring parents away serving in the military. I watched my students validate their own feelings and opinions, root themselves more deeply in their own convictions and beliefs, and come into their own a bit more. Being present for these projects and stories was an incredible experience and I viewed many of these adolescents in different lights after a deeper peek into their souls and psyches. I gained a much greater sense of who they were in that moment and was better equipped to meet individual student's musical and personal needs in my daily music classes.

SELF-ESTEEM

Self-esteem is related to how we feel about ourselves. It's not about how we actually look but how we feel about our looks. It's not about how smart we really are but how we feel about our intelligence. (Vermond 2013, 31)

The idea of self-esteem is often discussed in tandem with adolescence. Music education professor Thomas Regelski wrote in *Teaching General Music in Grades 4–8*, "students who possess a strong sense of identity are most confident and autonomous, conform less within the peer group and are most likely to be leaders" (Regelski 2004, 34). On the flip side, "Lack of an effective *sense of self* (e.g., insecurity, shyness) is associated with being socially isolated. Unpopularity and rejection often result in aggressive, demanding, and conceited behavior, or in compensatory attention seeking behavior" (ibid.).

Through self-esteem we evaluate ourselves and, as a result, maintain who we are. In the book *Building Self-Esteem in the Secondary School* (1991), Robert W. Reasoner and Gail Dusa specifically discussed self-esteem as one of the best things an adolescent can establish to prepare for life. With self-esteem comes an understanding and confidence in one's potential to succeed. Students with positive feelings about themselves are better able to determine personal goals, strengths, and weaknesses. In addition, adolescents with positive self-esteem are more open to new challenges and better equipped to cope with disappointments they may encounter.

Those who lack self-esteem commonly feel threatened by new challenges or see little success in their futures. Such students will avoid challenges and situations (perhaps by skipping class), depend on others to do assignments for them, and/or only apply minimal effort on work they complete themselves. Adolescents who lack self-esteem tend to be concerned with preserving some sense of self-respect or failing gracefully instead of putting forth more effort to succeed. These students will commonly strike out at teachers or make it a point to misbehave in class as a way of "saving face" in front of peers.

The idea of self-esteem holds important implications for us as music educators, because how our adolescent music students feel about themselves directly influences their personality and involvement with music. Activities naturally associated with music classes—from playing instruments to singing, composing, improvising, and reflecting—can be quite personal. If adolescent music students do not feel positive about themselves and their abilities, then they are less willing to be open to new musical challenges or "putting themselves out there." Positive self-esteem fosters a willingness to take risks and attempt new challenges, regardless of the possible outcomes.

The adolescent self-esteem continuum is wide-ranging, with overconfidence on one end and no confidence on the other. Our music students will continually find themselves at a variety of places on this continuum—even within a single day—influenced by what Kira Vermond calls "self-esteem zappers" in her book *Growing Up Inside and Out*.

> Just when you thought it was safe to look in the mirror without feeling crummy about yourself, guess what comes along? Self-esteem zappers! You'll know it when you come across them, too. They're the people, situations, and even ideas we encounter that make us second-guess who we are deep down. Maybe you've already come across them before....Girls aren't good at math. Boys don't cry. Girls don't play sports. Boys don't hug. Self-esteem zappers do a real number on kids growing up because that's the time when bodies, brains, and attitudes change. This means looking at the world around you and using that information to try to figure out who you are. If that information is positive and gels with how you feel about yourself, cool. You'll feel secure, healthy, and happy. But if it is negative or doesn't seem to reflect your personality or how you feel about the world, it can make things topsy-turvy and really uncomfortable. (Vermond 2013, 31–32)

Vermond goes on to address specific issues that may affect adolescent self-esteem by gender. For girls, she touches on body image, attractiveness, and the stereotype that girls are not good at math; for boys, she addresses popular stereotypes about boys (e.g., they're not supposed to cry, not supposed to be afraid, not supposed to ask for help), emotion, and acting tough. She poses questions for adolescents, such as: "What are the three words that best describe you? Are they positive or negative? Why?" These questions could easily be adapted for adolescent music students: "What are three words that best describe you as a [Musician? Singer? Instrumentalist? Songwriter? Arranger?] Are they positive or negative? Why?" She also suggests strategies toward developing self-esteem and acting like "the real you," all of which are beautifully transferrable to an adolescent music class setting (as I have demonstrated below) and should be discussed with students:

- *Try something new*: could be a new instrument, participation in a different music ensemble, or perhaps give composition a try!
- *Set a goal*: sing this piece by memory in two weeks, be selected for state honors band, raise $3,000 for the music booster program, or perform an original composition at the local coffee house mic night.
- *Stop beating yourself up!*: Vermond writes, "So what if you got a C- on your last test. It's possibly just a sign that you need to either study harder next time or ask for help. By the way, a lot of A-students aren't tomorrow's Einsteins. Some famous studies have shown that people who are really persistent (keep working at something even when they hit a big snag) are more likely to be successful than kids who give up sooner. In other words, while school obviously comes easy to some students, others study until they understand the material, even if it takes a long time. Something to think about. . . ." Therefore, emphasis on the musical process over product in our music classes can often combat adolescent self-depreciation about their music abilities and accomplishments, as well as increase self-esteem. In addition, an enthusiastic focus on the musical process in our classes often leads to an even more meaningful musical outcome.
- *Choose who you want to be:* Vermond writes, "I'm not going to tell you to "just be yourself." We've all heard that phrase a hundred times and is it ever all that helpful? If we all felt comfortable in our own skin, no one would be struggling with self-esteem! Instead, if you're going to compare yourself to other people and want to be like them, choose wisely. Find someone who already makes you feel confident and happy, not someone who makes you feel bad for failing to measure up . . .". Through our school music programs, we have access to younger and older music students, which can naturally lead to some sort of a music-mentoring program—not only for adolescent music students to be mentored, but also for them to mentor younger musicians. Such experiences have the potential to positively influence adolescent identity development and self-esteem. (Vermond 2013, 36)

With a little strategic effort, as music teachers we can contribute positively to students' musical and personal development as well as their involvement in more meaningful musical experiences. Because development of identity and self-esteem is not an overnight process, I feel like our work is analogous to that of someone painting a wall in their home: each time we revisit a topic or an idea, we put another coat of paint on the walls. Coat after coat, eventually we will end up with the wall color that we want; but in the meantime we have to be patient and let the paint dry between applications.

DIGEST

In this chapter we delved into a variety of adolescent characteristics that impact and influence our work as music educators, including details about physical nuances, emotional capacity, brain and cognitive development, identity formation, and self-esteem.

From understanding (or at least acknowledging) the range of potential factors that influence our adolescent students, we will more effectively meet their musical and developmental needs within our individual music classes.

At the beginning of this chapter, I encouraged you to recall your own adolescent experiences—both in connection to and beyond music—in efforts to form and retain personal perspective on adolescents. Did you find yourself gravitating towards positive memories or were your own adolescent experiences rooted in "storm and stress"? Perhaps a little of both? What are the implications of your experiences and reactions for your own teaching practice?

For those who are considering teaching an adolescent population of music students in the future, I encourage you to ponder the following questions and discuss them with others, both those who work with adolescent music students and those who do not.

- What positive outcomes do you feel are derived from the experience of adolescence? What positive experiences or outcomes do you recall about your own time in young adolescence?
- What fears or uncertainties do you have about working with an adolescent age group? What specifically makes you uncomfortable? What would it take for you to feel more comfortable with adolescents? What resources are available to you with regard to preparing for some of these uncertainties?
- What makes you excited about working with an adolescent music population? Of the topics in this chapter, about which do you feel optimistic for their potential to influence future young adolescents?

CHAPTER 2

The Music Teacher

Teachers know their lives in terms of stories. They live stories, tell stories of those lives, retell stories with changed possibilities, and relive the changed stories. We mean more than teachers telling stories of specific children and events. We mean that their way of being in the classroom is storied: As teachers they are characters in their own stories of teaching, which they author. (Clandinin and Connelly, 1995, 12)

We all have a story—many stories, actually. Stories of childhood and adolescence, stories of education and adulthood, or stories of family and friends—*all* of these stories, the good and the bad, influence who we are and how we approach teaching music to adolescents. Through awareness of the impact our stories have on us, we are better equipped to understand our beliefs and approaches to teaching music. For example, when I was a junior in college I did not have a strong sense of how to infuse my personality into my teacher persona. I distinctly remember sitting in the undergraduate music library, deep in personal crisis, as I realized that as a teacher *I had to be a grown-up*. And I completely freaked out because I did not know how I was going to do that and also be myself. I've always enjoyed being a bit quirky and silly; I like to make people laugh. But I wanted to teach high school, and all of the high school teachers I knew were refined, poised, elegant, and seemingly more mature than I thought I would ever be. Following graduation, I reluctantly began teaching young adolescents. However, the more time I spent with middle school students, the more I found that I could really, truly be myself—my quirky, goofy self—and I loved it.

One result of this personal experience was the solidification of my philosophy of teaching music to adolescents: I wanted my students to depart from our time together with a greater understanding of *themselves* through the study of music—their likes and dislikes, awareness of musicianship, tastes as consumers of music, and enhanced understanding of their place in the world. For me, music largely became a vehicle for unapologetic self-discovery and affirmation. Today as a music teacher educator, the core of my music education philosophy still holds true: I do not want my college students to be carbon copies of me or imitations of their high school music teacher. I want my students to figure out who *they* are as music educators and develop confidence to know that, fundamentally, the ways that they teach can work best for them regardless of how anyone else is doing it.

It is valuable for each of us to consider who we are and *why* we teach music to adolescents the ways that we do—whether we call this a philosophy, a belief system, or viewpoint—and realize how our personal and professional stories have influenced our approaches to the music classroom. Paulo Freire wrote in his book *Teachers as Cultural Workers: Letters to Those Who Dare to Teach* about teaching as an act of courage, commitment, and daring. I find the follow passage from this book to be invigorating and validating:

> The task of the teacher, who is also a learner, is both joyful and rigorous. It demands seriousness and scientific, physical, emotional, and affective preparation. It is a task that requires that those who commit themselves to teaching develop a certain love not only of others but also of the very process implied in teaching. It is impossible to teach without the courage to love, without the courage to try a thousand times before giving up. In short, it is impossible to teach without a forged, invented, and well-thought-out capacity to love. Here is how we make the link to the subtitle, *Letters to Those Who Dare Teach*. We must dare, in the full sense of the word, to speak of love without the fear of being called ridiculous, mawkish, or unscientific, if not antiscientific. We must dare in order to say scientifically, and not as mere blah-blah-blah, that we study, we learn, we teach, we know with our entire body. We do all of these things with feeling, with emotion, with wishes, with fear, with doubts, with passion, and also with critical reasoning. However, we never study, learn, teach, or know with the last only. We must dare so as never to dichotomize cognition and emotion. We must dare so that we can continue to teach for a long time under conditions that we know well: low salaries, lack of respect, and the ever-present risk of becoming prey to cynicism. We must dare to learn how to dare in order to say no to the bureaucratization of the mind to which we are exposed every day. We must dare so that we can continue to do so even when it is so much more materially advantageous to stop daring. (Freire, 2005, 5–6)

Therefore, consider your own storied life and music teaching career (thus far) for a moment. What has caused you to dare to be a music teacher? To be a teacher of adolescents? How did you arrive to where you are today? What stories have influenced your current path? Who has played a role in the various stories of your life? How have your stories and experiences influenced you and your approach to your music classroom? What do you believe about teaching adolescent musicians specifically, and why?

TEACHING YOUNG ADOLESCENTS

Curious as to how the contributing music educators came to teach middle school music, I asked them to share their stories; some of these were simple and some complex. However, regardless of where the teachers were in their careers at the time of our interviews, their individual stories aligned with each other through their great enjoyment of teaching adolescent musicians. I am honored to share some of them here.

To some degree reminding me of Goldilocks, Michelle (choir) felt that she did not quite "fit" with elementary students or with high school students. However, her fit with middle school music students was *just right*—especially as she found that they had the same sense of humor:

> MICHELLE: I want to be in that middle ground where you really start to inspire them and see that spark. You know, *I* started choir in sixth grade and it was *my* spark. I want to be that for these kids and start them on their journey. And then I started working with middle school singers and I realized that my maturity level was that of a middle schooler. So when I said "bus duty" and started laughing and the kids told me to grow up, I knew that I was teaching the right grade level.

In college, Tavia (band) had always intended to be a performer. She has two brass performance degrees and was all set to earn a third and teach college when injuries left her unable to play. While recovering, she decided that she wanted to teach high school band, so she completed her music education certification. During student teaching, she said, "I realized that middle school is where it's *at*. The kids are just so excited and they have this energy that high schoolers don't."

Also while student teaching, both Jason (band) and Gretchen (strings) realized how much they enjoyed middle school students. Jason was quite inspired by the work of his cooperating teacher: "I was amazed by the results and growth and the way that you can change kids so much at such an early age," he said. So he decided that middle school was where he wanted to stay. Gretchen had never intended to work in schools at all, but rather, planned to establish herself as a private string teacher. However, in the first five or six weeks of student teaching, she said, "I fell in love with middle school," and she has been teaching young adolescents since.

For James, his plan all along had been to be "God's gift to the high school world." He interviewed several times for high school choral positions, but was ultimately hired as an elementary music teacher. While teaching elementary music, James attended a middle school choral performance in his district. "I was blown away. I didn't know middle schoolers could make that kind of sound. I didn't know that they were capable of that kind of music making. And, I thought, 'Wow. I can do this.'" James eventually accepted a middle school choral position and over time has realized that the responsibilities associated with a high school choral position are no longer a good fit for him.

> JAMES: There were times when I wanted to go out and do high school choral stuff. But, frankly, I don't want the load. I don't want to do the musicals and everything else that comes with a high school job. So middle school is a good balance for me. I can do choral things that are pretty demanding. But at the same time, I don't have to be there day and night. I can still go hunting and fishing and play tennis and . . . all that other stuff.

When in college, David (choir and guitar) was a jazz guitar major. After seeing a performance of the American Boychoir School on tour, he "heard the call to be a music educator." The twist: not only did he now want to teach music, he wanted to teach *choral music*—in spite of having had no choral experience in high school or college. "That was kind of a big revelation for me at the time, because I was a guitar major," David said. After much hard work, most of David's renowned teaching career has involved teaching middle-level music, largely choir and guitar.

Some of these music educators had absolutely no interest in teaching middle school when they applied for positions, but ultimately ended up with the age group and then never left. When Kate (general) graduated from college, she promised herself that she would never teach middle school. In spite of this, following an interview for her current school district, she was assigned to teach at the middle school because she fit so well with the team of people already in place there. "So it was kind of an accident that I started teaching middle school," she said. Bethany (general) also described her landing a middle school position as accidental. Upon graduation from college, she applied to teach in a school district in Philadelphia.

> BETHANY: They give you a list of available positions and you just pick one. They had a big map up in the room so you could look where the jobs were and that's it. I said to some guy, "I want to be close to where I live." He looked at the map and said, "This is the best school close to your house, even though it's still pretty far." And I was like, "Okay!" So I picked it! (*chuckling*)

Deb (choir) was originally hired as an elementary music teacher, and her school district later added middle school choir to her teaching load.

> DEB: I was *really* scared because then I had to do sixth, seventh, and eighth grade choir. I mean, I'm musical, but I had no experience working with a mixed voice choir. Zero. It was really scary that first year.
> BRIDGET: So how do you feel about the middle school kids now?
> DEB: If I could write my job description right now I would teach at both middle schools, all choirs. Period.

Only Jay (choir and composition) specifically sought out a middle school teaching position "to get to know that level better." After five years of teaching both middle and high school students in various capacities, he realized that "middle school was a great level for me. I love the level. I love my job. I have been recruited by high schools, but I hope to retire from my middle school."

ROLES OF THE MUSIC TEACHER

We assume many roles as music educators, especially as our work with specific students can span across three or four consecutive school years. Consider all of the hats that you wear: What are the implications of each in your daily work? Which are the most rewarding? Which consume the most mental energy? Which use the most emotional energy? How do your various roles influence your students? How do your various roles influence or impact your own quality of life inside and outside of school?

Teaching can be very fulfilling, but also very exhausting. By occasionally taking stock of how your energy is "spent" in your days, you can keep a better tab on whether or not you are truly happy with your various roles.

And if not, what can be done to remedy the situation? Too many good teachers burn out as a result of unnecessarily spreading themselves across too many roles; they are exhausted physically, mentally, and emotionally from trying to meet the needs of many *other* people. The first person who truly deserves your energy is *you* (and you are no good to anyone if you are too frazzled), so be wary of playing every role for everyone else.

The next section of this chapter addresses some of the multifaceted roles commonly played by music teachers of adolescents. There are many, many roles that could be discussed in this book, but I have chosen to focus on the roles of music educator (including emphasis on enriching perspective on ourselves as music educators and providing meaningful musical opportunities), leadership, nurturer, cautious counselor, the role of teacher and not friend, and resourceful provider.

Music Educator Role

The mind, once stretched by a new idea, never returns to its original dimensions.
(Ralph Waldo Emerson [or Oliver Wendell Holmes])

Why teach adolescents about music? There is no quick and easy answer to this question, especially as we all have differences of opinion on why we teach music to adolescent students. However, let's begin with the fact that adolescents often do not have the words to fully express themselves. But, boy! Give them the opportunity to play a piece of music that demonstrates how they feel about something, or allow them to share the text of a song that expresses what they are experiencing, and their ability to nail it on the head can be just remarkable. Still, adolescents don't know what they don't know, and their understanding of music is limited by what they have learned thus far in their lives. By teaching students about music through performance, listening, conversation, analysis, dissection, demonstration, composition, and research, while also encouraging critical thinking, we provide them with ways to better understand why they feel the way they do and to more clearly communicate with others. Let's consider the intersection of opera and the adolescent—in my experience, not the most positive pairing, initially.

"I hate opera." *Do you really hate opera, or do you not understand opera? There's a difference.* "I don't like opera because it's slow." *Not all opera is slow ... let's take a closer look at a few things. . . . You say that you don't like opera because of the tempo of the music. Does that mean that you do not like any slow music?* "No. Opera is boring sounding. Not just because it's slow, I guess." *What do you prefer when you are listening to music?* "I like things to have a beat." *So, maybe you are not moved by opera because there is no hard beat—does that sound more accurate?* "Yeah, I guess."

From here you can take the conversation in a myriad of directions. For example, this student could learn about the intricate storytelling of musicals such as *Rent* or *In the Heights,* which happen to feature a strong beat throughout many of the songs and also include several slow songs. Ask the student about personal reactions to the use of beat in these contexts and why they feel the way they do. What are reactions to the slower songs and why? As *Rent* is a retelling of the story of the famous opera *La Boheme,* the student could compare and contrast storylines, settings, musical elements, use of dance, songs, performance practices, messages, and the histories of the two shows. Have the student consider the emotions that the music from both genres evokes for them. What specific musical elements elicit various emotions for the student and why? From here, discuss the student's preferences regarding stylistic or artistic facets of musical theater vs. opera. And so forth. . . While it is important that adolescent music students have opportunities to critically and objectively examine music, they also need to subjectively ponder its significance and contribution to the art world (and larger world) as well as how it impacts them, personally.

Then comes a really exciting part! As students gain the skills to dissect what they hear and perform and make distinctions about the various elements of their experiences, they are much more prepared to go forth and replicate musical experiences that they enjoy; intellegently discuss musical experiences that they have had; connect with other people in entirely new ways; and/or make more informed decisions about their involvement with or consumption of music. Ultimately, when our students are more aware of what evokes emotion for them in music and have a better understanding about their general musical likes and dislikes, they are more equipped to examine other experiences in their lives and figure out ways to express themselves in different capacities, as well as replicate or seek out specific musical experiences.[1]

As discussed in chapter one, we need to help our adolescent students move forward from our music lessons toward understanding how musical experiences are relevant to them in their own lives. So I want adolescent music students to leave a discussion about opera, or any musical idea, understanding more about the art form as well as why they feel the way they do. I want them to hear the opinions of their peers and feel validated and confident about their own feelings and reactions to the music, whether they completely align with the opinions of their peers or differ by 180 degrees. No more blanket statements such as, "I hate opera." I want my students to make informed decisions about their involvement with opera from our time together and move forward. Perhaps they will go forth excited about this art form! Maybe after our discussion they will explore other rock musical options, such as *Tommy* or *Hair* or *Memphis* as well as operas such as *Madame Butterfly* or *The Merry Widow*. Or maybe they will better understand some pop-culture reference five years down the road based on our conversation and, at that point in their life, a renewed interest in opera or musical theater will be ignited. Perhaps they will even understand their disinterest in stories that are sung and make an informed decision to spend time enjoying other activities or art forms. Any of these scenarios is possible, especially if our adolescent music students understand the motivations behind their musical decisions.

The quote at the beginning of this section—"The mind, once stretched by a new idea, never returns to its original dimensions"—is worth repeating again here. No matter what adolescent music students end up doing with the musical experiences and understandings we provide, whether in general music classes, ensemble rehearsals, or performance clinics and festivals, we should attempt to change the shape of their minds in some way. As music educators, it is part of our job to provide adolescent musicians with tools they can use as they go forth and make informed decisions about their interactions with music, ultimately ending up with a deeper understanding of themselves in the process.

Enriching Perspective on Ourselves as Music Educators

> Learning without reflection is a waste. Reflection without learning is dangerous.
> (Confucius)

Our role as music educator does not mean that we are exempt from the sorts of self-exploration that we ask from our students. In fact, efforts that provide opportunities for us to enrich and deepen our perspective about who we are as people, musicians, and music educators will only help us in our work with adolescent musicians. It is easy to put off reflection and contemplation about our own musical experiences because, let's face it, being a music educator is extremely busy work. However, *any* efforts to enrich perspectives on ourselves and our work with adolescent music students can pay off in huge dividends.

What follows are four activities of varying involvement to get you started on your contemplation journey. I also posed a number of questions in the beginning section of this chapter (on the influence of stories on our lives and work) and invite you to reflect upon these as well. Moving forward from this book, you are encouraged to seek out additional tasks, questions, and readings to help you continue to better understand who you are (or who you strive to be) as a musician and teacher—no matter how long you have been part of the music education profession—and use that enriched perspective to enhance and improve upon your teaching of adolescent music students. Be open to new curiosities and questions that arise for you during this process, and feel free to refer to the Confucius quote above for inspiration on your journey.

Activity #1: In my Music in Adolescence class at the University of Illinois, music education majors learn about teaching general music classes in middle and high school. At the beginning of the semester, we take some time to unpack our own adolesent experiences and complete a project called "Adolescent Me & Music," which is similar to the "Identity Music Project" discussed in chapter one. Students choose 4-6 one-minute snippets of songs that were influential to them during middle and/or high school and consider how each song affected, influenced, or supported them as a developing adolescent. In addition, during presentations of these snippets for the class, each person must share insight on how specific songs or circumstances surrounding the songs have impacted them as a future music educator. It is quite remarkable to hear the varied stories from my students, as well as their realizations of how important music was for them during this pivotal time of self-discovery in their lives, influencing who they are in present day.

If you embarked on such a project about your own adolescent years, what sorts of pieces would you choose to share and why? How have your own adolescent experiences and interactions with music informed your work today as a middle-level music educator? Consider the implications of what you have realized about yourself on your future work as a music teacher of adolescents–how will your teaching beliefs and practices be tweaked or reinforced? To further enrich the experience, complete this project this with a friend or two and share/compare. What did you find? How were your adolescent experiences similar and/or different? What are the implications of these similarities and/or differences within your different schools or the broader music education profession?

Activity #2: Also as part of my Music in Adolescence class, my college music students are required to keep a listening journal following criteria put forth by music education professor Maud Hickey in her book *Music Outside the Lines: Ideas for Composing in K-12 Music Classrooms.* The lesson instructions are as follows:

> Use this journal to keep a list of all of the music you hear during the day. Each day write the titles (or description if you do not know the title) of music you

hear during the day, and the place you are when you hear it. Choose one piece that is your favorite and one that is your least favorite from the week to describe in more detail. Use the format below for your descriptions:

> Favorite (least favorite) music title:
> Composer/artist:
> Describe the musical elements:
> What musical elements make this piece your favorite (least favorite)?
> What personal elements make this piece your favorite (least favorite)?
> Share these through class discussions. (Hickey 2012, 59)

Following this activity, my college students are always surprised at what they learn about their musical preferences and responses to the music they have heard, as well as about themselves after having studied music for several years. Four of them granted me permission to share excerpts of their reflections here, which provide evidence of their thinking processes and moments of self-discovery through this activity.

OVERALL THOUGHTS: I started to think a lot about my listening habits in high school. I realized that a lot of other people listen to more music than I do, and that I seemed to be lacking in a number of "must-know" songs. This project reinforced my realization that I prefer to focus on one artist or album at a time and take a long time to really pick apart what they have created. I love Bon Iver's album, and have had it for several months, but I have yet to come to solid conclusions on what many of the lyrics mean. Without the liner notes, I still have a hard time picking out lyrics. I do know that I seek out atmosphere and layers in the music I listen to, and I tend to like either really mellow music or very intense music. For whatever reason, the in-between can only be filled by something that really interests me in its construction. I would love to use this project to get to know some of my future students' listening habits and perhaps discuss them in my future classrooms. (Syrus White, junior music education major)

LEAST FAVORITE: "Back in Black"—ACDC
Among the list of musical works listed above this one stands out as distinctly different from the other selections, and that is because this is one of my sister's recordings she played for me on the drive back to the University of Illinois. She and I have opposite musical tastes, and based on other selections she has played for me I decided I wasn't going to like this one before she even played it,

strictly because it was "her" music. Personally I also just don't like anything too harsh, and I can't stand anything that's not melodic in any sense, and to me the vocals just sounded non-musical.

Musically I didn't like how bare the accompaniment was; though the guitar part is extremely famous I thought that overall the entire recording (though loud and brash) was fairly empty. The tone of the guitar and the vocals were both extremely rough and I thought that both sounded like they were competing for the attention of the song; neither seemed to be the focus. I also thought that the song remained fairly stagnant. There was no musical growth besides the guitar solo, and I felt musically bored throughout the entire recording (so we switched back over to my music while my sister put in her headphones). (Megan Warren, junior music education major)

FAVORITE: "If I Didn't Believe in You"

COMPOSER/ARTIST: From the musical *The Last Five Years* by Jason Robert Brown

What musical elements made this piece your favorite?

The singer was incredibly expressive in his performance of the song, "If I Didn't Believe in You." The piece tells a story about a married couple who is on the verge of breaking up. If I were to read the text without listening to the music, I would still be moved because the text tells a beautiful, but sad, story. The music enhances the text and provides its own expressive qualities.

In the beginning of the song, the husband (and soloist) is describing a prolonged fight that the couple is experiencing. The chorus however, is much more hopeful as the husband explains all of the reasons that he believes in his wife. Personally, I feel that even the way the title is worded is important to the story. The title is "If I Didn't Believe in You" and the husband lists several things he would do if he did not believe in his wife. Throughout the piece, the husband is defending himself, not convincing his wife that he believes in her. His tone is condescending and competitive. The couple does not end up together in the end, which is why the title of the piece is not "I Believe in You." The husband never explicitly states that he believes in his wife.

The piano reflects the stagnant nature of the piece. The husband is trying to convince his wife that they should be together, but his attempts are futile. The piano mirrors this lack of motion through a motive that occurs several times throughout the song. This motive begins with the tonic in the low bass and high soprano on half notes, then the moving line begins on the mediant in the middle range, but it ultimately ends back where it started on the mediant. The stagnant notes create a frame, while the suspension on the mediant and subdominant create a sense of hopeful longing that is also expressed in the text.

The range of the piece is higher at the climax of the song and the dynamic becomes louder. Both of these elements heighten the emotions being expressed. The climax is abruptly ended when the soloist sings a powerful line, followed by a strong and meaningful silence. The song ends with one final repetition of the motive. (Katie Bruton, junior music education major)

FAVORITE ALERT!: Solas Ane—Samuel Hazo

HOLY MOLY YESYESYESYESYES I listened to this like fifteen times after I was done observing at Glenbard East High School. Gorgeous band piece based on an Irish melody—name means "Yesterday's Joy" and is perfectly evoked by the different brass/ woodwind sections weaving in and out. Woodwinds have solo-ish, exposed, delicate sections, and the band played them so well in-tune and emotionally and YES.

I probably love this piece because it's incredibly lyrical, captures emotion in the perfect way that words often can't, and shows that a) brass instruments sound AWESOME when dialed back dynamically and given sweeping lines and b) woodwind feature sections played well are fantastically gorgeous. (Meghan Jain, junior music education major)

You are strongly encouraged to explore Hickey's book, try this activity, and take a good look at your own listening reponses. What do you discover about your own reactions to different kinds of music and, most importantly, *why* do you feel the way that you do? What musically moves you? For me, through such activities I've gained a better understanding of why I enjoy music from Jack White, Alabama Shakes, Foo Fighters or Dave Matthews so much—it's their juxaposition of harsh sections with beautiful melodic or harmonic moments that engage and intrigue me. From such personal contemplations, I've come to realize how much I enjoy music that is more raw, unpolished, and soulful. I realize that I am much more appreciative of musicians who mix contrasting elements in their music and who build tension and then resolve it in their music.

Going even further down the rabbit hole, I have also gained a better understanding of how my musical preferences influence the choral music that I choose when working with middle and high school singers, as well as the musical elements I choose to highlight for them during our time together. With this understanding, I now feel more grounded in my choices of choral repertoire because I better understand *why* I am drawn to different pieces of music (and why I shy away from others). As a result, I am better at balancing the different kinds of music that I choose for singers and am much more thoughtful and deliberate in my selections.

Ultimately, by more deeply understanding the elements of music that evoke emotion for me, I have become a more informed musician, consumer of music, choral teacher, and conductor, and have developed my ability to discuss, appreciate, experience, enjoy, and share all music on entirely new levels—even after being an experienced musician for many, many years.

Activity #3: Robert Brooks invites participants in his workshops to engage in a brief exercise to deepen their understanding of themselves as teachers. He first asks those in attendance to describe ideal and less-than-ideal teachers, and then poses the following scenario:

> Imagine for a moment that I ask all of you to leave and I call in the students you teach. I then request your students to use one or more words to describe you. What words would you hope they use? What words do you think they would use? What images do you think are important to project as a teacher? If we could see the world through your students' eyes, what images would be cast?" (Brooks, 1991, 19)

Consideration of your teaching practice through the imagined perspective of your students can be very insightful, especially if done in a frank and honest manner. How would you respond to Brooks's questions? Are you pleased with your responses? If no, what changes would you make in your classroom with regard to teaching practice, policies, and/or interactions with others? If yes, what would you keep the same and why?

Activity #4: Following guidelines from the This I Believe organization, you are encouraged to create a statement with the intent of addressing the theme of "This I Believe: Teaching Adolescents Music." The following guidelines come from the original invitation to complete a "This I Believe" statement on a topic of their choice (http://thisibelieve.org/history/invitation/):

- This invites you to make a very great contribution: nothing less than a statement of your personal beliefs, of the values which rule your thought and action. Your essay should be about three minutes in length when read loud, written in a style as you yourself speak, and total no more than 500 words.

- We know this is a tough job. What we want is so intimate that no one can write it for you. You must write it yourself, in the language most natural to you. We ask you to write in your own words and then record in your own voice. You may even find that it takes a request like this for you to reveal some of your own beliefs to yourself. If you set them down they may become of untold meaning to others.
- We would like you to tell not only what you believe, but how you reached your beliefs, and if they have grown, what made them grow. This necessarily must be highly personal. That is what we anticipate and want.
- It may help you in formulating your credo if we tell you also what we do not want. We do not want a sermon, religious or lay; we do not want editorializing or sectarianism or "finger-pointing." We do not even want your views on the American way of life, or democracy or free enterprise. These are important but for another occasion. We want to know what you live by. And we want it in terms of "I," not the editorial "We."
- We do ask you to confine yourself to affirmatives: This means refraining from saying what you do not believe. Your beliefs may well have grown in clarity to you by a process of elimination and rejection, but for our part, we must avoid negative statements lest we become a medium for the criticism of beliefs, which is the very opposite of our purpose.

My music education students complete a "This I Believe: Teaching Adolescents Music" statement at the end of my Music in Adolescence class. It has proven to be a valuable experience in helping them solidify their opinions and philosophies about music in the lives of adolescent students in a positive and proactive way. Although the actual details of this task are few, the resulting thinking is quite deep; the resulting project is very concise; and the ramifications of such self-exploration are far-reaching.

Through activities such as the four outlined above (and there are many others out there just as valuable), we will challenge, enrich, and validate our thinking and beliefs about teaching adolescents while solidifing our philosophies of music education and deepening our own future experiences with music and teaching. In addition, they provide excellent opportunities for potential collaboration and connection with other music educators that often come too far and few between.

Providing Meaningful Musical Opportunities

Part of our role as a music educator is to be a conduit between adolescent music students and meaningful music experiences—both inside and outside of our own classrooms. A *big* part of our job is getting our music students fired up about the many possibilities of musical involvement and recognizing the meaningfulness of their musical experiences. In Mike's (band) own words:

> MIKE: I almost feel an obligation to give them as many opportunities as possible, whether it be something as simple as picking quality music or taking them to high-quality festivals or on trips. You know, we want everything musical to be memorable so they're hooked! So they love music! And that will translate to them playing in high school and college. And even if they don't play past high school, they'll still say, "Oh man! I still love this jazz song" or "I still love this trumpeter that I listened to on a CD when I was in seventh grade and it's still something that I enjoy."

In my first years of teaching middle school choir, I felt pressured to teach students in ways that would prepare them for their time in high school choir. I eventually came to the realization that whatever happened beyond my classroom was really out of my control, so why was I spending so much energy in that direction? While students were with *me*, I should give them everything I could to send them forth as intelligent consumers of music and thoughtful world citizens, regardless of whether they ever took another music class. This shift in my energies resulted in my being much less worried about the unknown musical future of my students and increased my enjoyment of work in the classroom. Both Gretchen (strings) and Andrew (strings) shared similar sentiments.

> GRETCHEN: I see myself as introducing music to students and getting them excited about music. I don't think we should be trying to convince kids at age ten or eleven that they need to be a professional musician. I think that they need an opportunity to experience music and experience *different* kinds of music, so I try really hard to teach all forms of music. I do baroque teaching, I do classical teaching, I do fiddle music, I do jazz music, I do pop music—I feel like they need to be introduced to all of these. When you foster that love for music, it becomes easier to get them to try something else that they wouldn't try originally. The whole goal that I have for being a teacher is to help them become what I call "functional musicians" (that's just a term that I've made up over the years). A functional musician to me is somebody that can appreciate music later in life. They can go to a concert or be a patron of the

arts in some form, or they can go jam with their friends and play whatever instrument they choose. Or they might just hear a song on the radio or hear a song on the Internet, look up the music to it and teach it to themselves. I want to give them enough skills so they can go further in whatever route they choose.

ANDREW: Music is very much the thing that can give students a sense of accomplishment, awareness, eloquence and maturity. I would say most of these kids might not grow up to be professional musicians, so it's my job to help them find a voice and develop a sense of appropriate interaction, self-expression, and positive influence on the world around them.

Our role as "music educator" is really quite special in that we are not just developing musical skills, we are making connections for adolescent students across the board—psychologically, emotionally, physiologically, socially—through all of the musical experiences that we provide. We accomplish this through the topics we choose, including the repertoire we select, the artists we feature, and so forth, as well as by honoring each adolescent's unique relationship with music. "I don't think the subject matters too much as long as connections can be made to the emotions, the historical context, the musical style, and such" (Jay, choir and composition). To illustrate how making such connections for adolescent music students might look in real time, let's consider musical experiences facilitated by David (choir and guitar) and Robyn (strings).

As part of his choral program, David regularly provides large- and small-group opportunities for his adolescent singers to musically model for each other, with the goals of developing musical skills as well as a sense of self-concept. "I feel like a lot of what I try to do is to build efficacy in students through mastery experiences and a classroom environment in which people can sing for each other and perform for each other." Individuality is greatly honored and, through performances for each other, students "become aware of what another person is doing; someone who has a similar age and similar abilities to them."

DAVID: I leave some time every week on Friday for this, even if it's just the last fifteen or twenty minutes at the end of the day. They can come up and sing anything they want, even a pop song (as long as it's school-appropriate). *Anything* that they are feeling because, you know, these students—and adolescents, in general—most of them have a very rich musical life outside of school. In fact, some students' in-school musical lives are really quite small compared to their out-of-school musical lives. So one of the best things I can do is to build bridges and lure out the distinctions between those two worlds. I feel like these activities help get rid of those inhibitions to not sing for each other, but it also helps them to see that I'm interested in their out-of-school musical lives. I also think that it helps them to see the relevance of musical values that I'm trying to impart to them, so that they don't just see music so compartmentalized to "in-school music" and "out-of-school music."

As David is very thoughtful about providing opportunities for his students to connect vocal music experiences and self-concept development, Robyn is very thoughtful about immersion experiences she arranges for her string students. She very much wants them to experience orchestra in a multitude of ways. As an example, she arranged for Mark Wood, the lead violinist of the Trans-Siberian Orchestra, to conduct a district-wide festival with sixth, seventh, and eighth grade orchestra students. Her words are much more compelling than my paraphrasing, so I will let Robyn speak about this experience:

ROBYN: And for two days we worked on just this rock and roll music— "Born to Be Wild," "A String Thing," "We Will Rock You." We used electric music instruments at our school and the kids had the opportunity to *rock out*. "Oh my gosh, this can exist! We don't have to play the '1812 Overture' every single year. We can actually learn to rock!" And it was a huge eye-opening experience for a lot of those kids, especially for the ones who may be on the verge of dropping because they have this preconceived notion that orchestra music only equals classical music. Now we're throwing this at them and it was just mind-blowing.

It is really important to start them young and make impressions like this on them. I went to concerts as a kid and that memory sticks with me. Or bringing in people like Mark Wood or Randy Sabien, an incredible jazz violinist—when I was a student teacher, he did workshops with our middle school kids and taught them another way to explore on their string instruments. Why not, within music, show students what else is out there? For example, a school near mine has an all-Baroque ensemble with all Baroque instruments. If that appeals to you, you can go that route; or if you take an electronic music class, you can go that route. So at the middle school level, I think it's our responsibility to introduce all of these things to our students and let them see what is possible.

Consider your own music classroom, either the one in which you currently work or the one you envision for your future. In what sorts of varied ways do you (or could you) encourage your students' musical involvement, both within and outside of your music program? How are students' musical endeavors overtly discussed or celebrated in your classroom? In what ways are students encouraged to recognize the meaningfulness of their musical experiences (both in-school and out-of-school experiences)? Do you share stories with your students about your own meaningful music experiences beyond your classroom?

As we move forward to consider other roles we play as music educators, I would like to leave the present discussion with a very poignant quote from Jay (choir and composition):

> JAY: At this level, making music is unlike many other curricular and noncurricular activities in that it is not a competition. It is not a race to the top. It is not an every-man-for-himself scenario against a standardized test where it doesn't matter if the student next to you fails, as long as you pass, it's okay. This is a unique chance to work together, feel together, emote together, create together, and more. They will remember those feelings of brotherhood and synchronicity and hopefully want to come back to it.

Leadership Role

In 1929, American philosopher and renowned educational reformer John Dewey described the history of school programs as a swinging pendulum. At one end of the pendulum swing was the school setting of authoritarianism, strict regulation, and rules. At the opposite end of the pendulum swing was the nonstructured school setting designed to allow students to develop from within. Dewey openly criticized educational systems that switched between extreme educational settings way back in 1929. Yet still today the pendulum often gets "stuck" at one end of the swing, where the approach is overdone, rather than staying in constant motion to maintain a balance of ideas. Case in point: the current extreme focus on standardized testing in schools.

However, in more recent years, a shift in the music education profession has encouraged more student-centered, democratic music classrooms (figure 2.1) and a move away from "traditional" music classrooms of dictatorship or authoritarianism (figure 2.2).

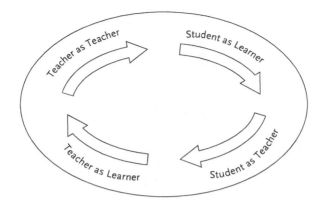

Figure 2.1 Student-centered, democratic music classroms.

Figure 2.2 "Traditional" music classrooms of dictatorship or authoritarianism.

Goals of a more student-centered, democratic music class are to musically, intellectually, and emotionally empower students and raise awareness of the impact students can have on others. According to music education professor Paul Woodford, educating music students about (and towards) democratic goals will only benefit society.

> Above all, democracy depends on the existence of good faith and generosity of spirit, of character and love for one's fellow men and women. These kinds of virtues are the glue that can bind us together as a society, for they motivate conversation and the forging of relationships leading to a sense of community. (Woodford 2005, 84)

Along the same lines, in her article "Teaching Music as Democratic Practice," music education professor Lisa DeLorenzo stressed the importance of music learning environments that not only adhered to musical standards, but also provided opportunities for students to problem solve, practice fairness, and gain knowledge of social justice through the arts that would impact and improve their musical experiences.

Bringing these ideas into the realm of our current and future work in adolescent music education, consider the following: What is the current environment of your music classroom versus your ideal vision for your music classroom? In what ways are more student-centered, democratic principles—such as musically, intellectually, and emotionally empowering students and raising awareness of the impact students can have on others—involved in the environment of your music classroom? And lastly, how do you identify yourself with your students? As a *teacher*? *Conductor*? *Director*? *Conductor/Teacher*? Specific words such as these can be linked to different philosophies of working with adolescent music students and manifest in a variety of ways in the classroom, some more student-centered than others. Let's take a closer look at official definitions of the first three words (courtesy of www.merriam-webster.com):

TEACHER: a person or thing that teaches something; *especially*: a person whose job is to teach students about certain subjects.
CONDUCTOR: a person who stands in front of people while they sing or play musical instruments and directs their performance.
DIRECTOR: a person who supervises the production of a show (as for stage or screen) usually with responsibility for action, lighting, music, and rehearsals.

What are the implications of these definitions for our work in the adolescent music classroom? Clearly there are differences in definitions for all three words, especially with regard to a teacher-centered versus a student-centered focus. Now, none of the definitions implicitly state that "teacher" automatically guarantees a more student-centered approach to the classroom but, generally, these definitions imply that "conductor" and "director" involve a more teacher-centered approach to the music classroom.

Next, consider the idea of identifying as a "conductor/teacher" in your music classroom, which is a term deliberately used by choral conductor and music educator, Sandra Snow, on her DVD *Choral Conducting/Teaching: Real World Strategies for Success*. Her definition for the term:

CONDUCTOR/TEACHER: emphasis is placed on pedagogy while upholding the expectations for artistry, embedded in the word "conductor." (Snow, 2009)

Although the ideas in Snow's DVD are intended specifically for choral music educators and choral conductors, the characteristics on which she focuses for conductor/teachers are easily transferrable to multiple and various music teaching and learning settings for adolescent students. Consider the following characteristics of Snow's conductor/teacher with regard to your own work as a music educator, regardless of musical area or medium:

- Employs enhanced methods of listening that involve hearing more and imposing less
- Completes score analysis with a thoughtful system; utilization of the score analysis as the basis of planning and conducting effective rehearsals
- Acknowledges context, which utilizes a fluid pedagogical approach for various situations and considers singers' skills and experiences, social factors, and learning styles
- Adapts; willing to abandon teaching strategies that are not working; to redirect, redeploy, extend, refine, and change rehearsal approach; to base decisions on in-the-moment, ongoing assessments of what the students are actually doing;
- Improvises; brainstorms, in real time, multiple teaching strategies designed to increase understanding of ensemble members; based upon a rich knowledge of teaching, improvisation encourages students' continual growth
- Facilitates; is an agent of change on the podium with a specific emphasis on development of musical thinking by ensemble members; includes a vast array of tools, including nonverbal and verbal strategies to stimulate critical thinking. (Snow, 2009)

Of key importance to the conductor/teacher approach is the intentionality that is encouraged during planning and teaching to acknowledge the many differences among musicians through a focus on accommodating students' varied skills, experiences, social factors, and learning styles. As discussed throughout chapter 1 of this book, adolescents are constantly changing in all kinds of ways; each adolescent is unique and must be approached on a case-by-case basis. The idea of a conductor/teacher in the adolescent music classroom makes great sense, as it involves taking into account all of the adolescent unpredictability (especially with regard to skill, experiences, social factors, and learning styles) on a daily basis and using it as an advantage, rather than a detriment.

All of this said, it is not wrong to refer to you as a teacher, conductor, director, or even a conductor/teacher. However, what *is* important is recognizing and acknowledging the differences between these words and the implications they each hold for practice and performance. Our work as *music educators* is to educate adolescents about music in all sorts of ways, shapes, and forms—regardless of ensemble or general music class format. And although I am a huge proponent for the terms "conductor/teacher" and "student-centered teaching," I acknowledge that I have seen many successful approaches within a variety of teaching settings with different groups of students and an array of music educators. It truly boils down to the individual philosophy of each music teacher. I no longer believe that there is one "best way" to teach adolescents music. Case in point: let us take a look at Deb (choir), Seth (choir), Gretchen (strings), and Michelle (choir), who are each extraordinary adolescent music educators but approach teaching their students in very different ways.

Deb maintains a very student-centered but authoritative approach to her middle school choral classroom and truly upholds a no-tolerance policy for anything but respectful behavior.

> DEB: *(a coy smile on her face)* The kids will tell you, it is a *loving* dictatorship. Don't like it? *Not* a problem! Go take shop! Go do another class. It's not a democracy. *Nobody* will love them like me, but *my* class, thank you. I'm the boss. The only classroom rule I have is "You are required to show respect" and that's *all* that it takes. That's respect for the stuff and respect for the people. I have to follow the same exact rule that you do. I *have* to be respectful of you. Do I have to like you? No. But I do. Do you have to like me? No, but you'd better show me respect. If that doesn't work for you, I respect that . . . get out of here.

Deb's high expectations of students—both musically and personally—are key to the success of her students and her choral program. At the same time, her students adore her and she has fostered a welcoming and safe classroom culture. Students advance from her choir program as confident, independent musicians as well as supported, loved, and more compassionate people. Interestingly, Deb's students leave her program embracing and embodying democratic outcomes, even though they were accomplished in an authoritatively run music classroom.

Seth's approach to his middle school choirs resembles that of Deb—authoritatively run with an emphasis on democratic goals—evident in the following comment when asked about his role in his music classroom:

> SETH: There is no democracy; this is an absolute dictatorship! My role is to show them through demonstration, through talking to them, through everything else, how to be in life. This goes beyond

singing. I want them to learn from me how to act in society. How to be good citizens as well as good musicians.

On the contrary, the following comments by Gretchen and Michelle indicate that these two teachers operate their classrooms quite differently than Deb and Seth. Their approaches to teaching are firmly rooted in stories from their own experiences as music students and follow a more student-centered, democratic approach to teaching adolescents.

GRETCHEN: I'm the conductor, but I'm not the only musician in the room. I can veto ideas but I do want to hear everybody else's idea of how they think a musical piece should go. As we get further along, I am more of a guide than anything; I'm there to bounce ideas off of. I try to let them figure out what they think a piece should be like in the beginning and then I'll bring in a recording or I'll bring in some perspective, either historical or just my own insight on things. When I was younger I did not like when a music teacher just walked in and told me, "This is how it should be because I said so." The world doesn't work like that anymore.

MICHELLE: I am a facilitator of music education. I am not a dictator, although I do tell the kids when they say (in a whiny voice), "That's not fair!" I'll say, "I'm sorry. This is a monarchy and I am queen." You know, so I'll use that line. But really, my music education was so forced that I have no idea how I became a music teacher. My elementary teacher, my middle school . . . it was just yell yell yell. You will sing this! It was just so authoritarian. We had no decisions. It was not the way I want to be. And I'm not saying that I'm a pot-smoking hippie or anything like (in a high, fluty voice), "I want my kids to make their own decisions," but I feel like I can give the kids a guideline and they can choose within that. And they still feel like they have ownership.

The bottom line here is that there is no "right" way to teach music to adolescents but, rather, everything is contextual. Consider all of the factors discussed in chapter 1 that contribute to the complexity of the adolescent music student—bodies growing sporadically, brains developing around a myriad of experiences, emotions coloring all situations, the emergence of identity and self-esteem, navigation of musical skills, and much more—and all of this happening at different rates for each student. There simply is no one-size-fits-all way to teach this population. The great part is that *you* get to decide what approach works best for your music students within your own unique teaching situation, as well as what works best for you.

Nurturer Role

During my years as a middle school choir teacher I worked with students from all walks of life. Some of my students were raised in home environments with a strong family core; others were raised in appalling home situations or were literally homeless. Students' stories ran the gamut—they thrilled me, fascinated me, amused me, and horrified me. As a result, I worked hard to be a constant positive adult figure in my adolescent students' lives. I wanted them to know that—regardless of who they were and whatever their home circumstances—I was rooting for them.

With regard to home life, in 1968 Arthur Thomas Jersild published some very poignant comments about adolescents that still hold true today. He wrote that continued assurance of parents' love is invaluable during adolescent years, especially when there are no worries about how to *keep* their parents' love. As a result, adolescents tend to trust their parents (even in times of disagreement) and gain a sense of security that allows greater freedom to explore, to investigate, and to be themselves. In addition, parental love helps adolescents feel that they can make mistakes without always worrying about fatal consequences. However, as Jersild points out, parental love is not a shield against disappointments, errors of judgment, weaknesses, or does it guarantee good conditions at school, work, and other places. And although many children are fortunate to grow within a loving household, "evidence seems to show that many adolescents who are having a hard time come from an unfavorable home background" (Jersild 1968, 241). Adolescents raised within unfavorable circumstances must work to find affection and approval from adult figures outside of their homes and, often without readily available encouragement or guidance, must depend upon their own resources.

In today's society, an uncomfortably high percentage of students come from homes without adequate support, encouragement, or role models, which are "vital during the very early adolescent years because this is the time when identity begins to take shape" (Gerber 1994, 7). According to Csikszentmihalyi and McCormack (1986), the few hours that students spend with teachers each day are the most important opportunities for them to learn from adults in our culture. "Our culture has essentially delegated the upbringing of its young to educational institutions" (Csikszentmihalyi and McCormack 1986, 417). As a middle school choir teacher, I certainly felt this "unofficial charge" from society to make a difference in my students' lives above and beyond any musical training they received. Several of the middle school teachers to whom I spoke also felt a sense of duty to teach more than music, including Jay (choir and composition):

JAY: The longer I teach, the more I realize my role. My job is not just to teach them to sing well, read music, or perform. My job is use choral music as a means to teach them how to work hard and learn, teach themselves, work well with others, and expect the best from themselves. Beyond that, my job is to create opportunities for them to build and exercise strong character traits, and experience feelings and learn from them. Some include: the joy of success, the pride of a job well done as the result of hard work, memorable social experiences with friends, sympathy and love for others, dedication, perseverance, responsibility, moral fortitude, being open-minded, being tolerant of others and accepting them, and being a good person in general. Think of the character-building and teamwork-building activities one might do at camp or at a workshop. The activity teaches the character trait. For some teachers, it's sports, dance, yearbook, scouting, and so on. Our activity is music. Always music.

Playing all of the roles that our many students need in their varied lives is an impossible goal, but we can still be an importance presence for our adolescent musicians. Remember that sometimes small and simple acts of kindness can make a huge difference to adolescent students during their daily comings and goings. For example, adolescents will certainly let *you* know that you are noticed—what you wear, what you drive, where you buy your groceries, when you look under the weather (my favorite)—it is how adolescents show that they care. In return, it is important that we notice *them* as well, which can help them feel good about themselves. Michelle (choir) used interactions with her students to build them up in all kinds of little ways that ultimately made big impacts. One of her stories:

MICHELLE: We had this one little girl, Hillary, and she was as quiet as a mouse. I had her for three years and she is in the top choir and works really hard. She's just really, really quiet. I deemed her "The Ninja." So if something happened, you know like sometimes the lights would flicker and I'd look at her and say, "You know, Hillary . . . *really*? We're in class." And she would grin and everyone would laugh; she loved it! She got some positive reinforcement, some social pull . . . you know, and people paid attention to her. It was a big deal for her.

In my own music classroom, if I thought something nice about one of my students I always made it a point to actually *tell* that student what I was thinking. "I really like that color on you!" "What a great smile you have!" "You look quite dapper today—what's the occasion?" I once overheard two of my middle school students talking about me: "She is the only teacher who ever notices that I get my hair cut." I considered that *quite* the compliment and continue the practice today with whomever I'm around.

In addition to nurturing our adolescent students on an emotional level, part of our work as music teachers is to also nurture our students' musical skills. The adolescent music classroom is a perfect setting to observe nature versus nurture at work. As discussed in chapter 1, during the specific years that we work with our adolescent music students, they are undergoing a tremendous amount of physical, emotional, and cognitive change; the "nature" piece of adolescent development is largely underway, operating on its own schedule for each individual adolescent. However, at the crossroads of physical development and desire for specialization (again, as discussed in chapter 1) our work must involve nurturing student musical development so that musical accomplishments are experienced and acknowledged (no matter how small) and students feel confident about their musical abilities. Otherwise, nature alone will solely influence students' decisions about their present and future musical involvement.

Cautious Counselor Role

The teacher role of "nurturer" can sometimes become intertwined with the role of "counselor." In the book *Counseling Skills for Teachers,* Jeffrey Kottler and Ellen Kottler wrote, "Whether or not you like it, whether you prepare for the role or not, you will be sought out as a confidante by children who have nowhere else to turn" (2007, 2). Of course we should be kind to distraught students; however, it is imperative to remember that we are not trained counselors. We are trained and licensed music educators, happy to be there for adolescent music students who need a shoulder to cry on or have a victory to celebrate. However, we have no business *counseling* our students in a variety of serious personal situations.

As teachers of adolescents, it is not uncommon for us to have students who learn about their parents' divorce or the death of a family member as they are dropped off at school in the morning. Or two best friends are suddenly friends no more. Perhaps a student's parent is abusing drugs, or a student is being badly bullied by a family member or a friend, struggling with his or her sexuality; or has not eaten in twenty-four hours. Sadly, music students often deal with situations that take personal precedence over their schooling. Therefore, it is imperative that, as music teachers, we do our best to recognize when our students need extra support or guidance. Keep on the lookout for warning signs such as changes in student mood, attitude, or work habits; self-destructive behaviors; cutting or signs of substance abuse; and so forth. If anything seems suspect, it is best to protect our students and ourselves by utilizing resources available by way of school counselors, administrators, and social workers.

The Role of Teacher, Not Friend

In nurturing or cautiously counseling students, whether personally or musically, adolescents can sometimes get a little confused about our role with them—often this happens when students are experiencing moments of lower self-esteem or are feeling a bit vulnerable (maybe their friend was mean to them; we are kind to them) or in moments of great jubilation (their crush finally asked them to the dance; they tell us and we get excited for them). However, during their formative years, adolescents need us to be their role model and not their friend. Gretchen (strings) remarked that "first, students understand that I am an adult and they're the students and that we're not going to be friends. It's just not going to be that way." However, she does share aspects of her personal life with students that pertain to classroom topics of conversation. For example, "I have two younger siblings who are both musicians. They are great fiddlers, so I bring them in to play music once a year for the kids, who can ask questions." Jason (band) also commented on maintaining a teacher role with his students: "My relationship with my students is that of teacher and student. Crossing the boundary as a friend can lead to much difficulty and will be counterproductive, educationally."

There is a difference between being friendly and being friends with our adolescent music students. From my own experiences, I acknowledge that adolescents can come across as mature and responsible young adults able to carry on mature, adult-like conversations. The juxtaposition of this side of them with their goofy nature is one of my favorite aspects of the age group. However, it is in those moments of maturity that the line could be blurred between teacher and friend, creating challenges in maintaining teacher authority. To prevent such problems in your music program, consider proactive steps such as the following guidelines put forth by the University of Oregon Teaching Effectiveness Program (TEP):

- One of the best ways to maintain authority is to have good teaching and classroom management skills. If you are new to teaching, get some assistance in planning your lessons and go for a more structured approach in the beginning until you feel you have enough information about your students to handle them differently.
- Be well prepared and organized for each class. If you teach large groups, your presentation skills are very important. If you spend the majority of class time lecturing, your ability to engage and maintain your students' attention will be critical.
- Establish your credentials on the first day. Talk about your background and your particular areas of expertise. You will be able to offer them valuable guidance and if there are questions you cannot answer, you will quickly help them find a good resource.
- Be clear about your expectations. If you want to enforce certain policies regarding attendance, late assignments, missed exams, etc., be clear and concise and have these things included on your syllabus or information sheet that is handed out at the beginning of the term. If you want students to sit near the front, ask them to do this right away. Don't wait a week or more after seating patterns have been established.
- Consider how you dress as a possible factor in how students respond to you. An overly casual appearance may undermine your credibility—at least on the surface. It's important that you are comfortable and dressing up a bit in the beginning can sometimes help.
- The more you begin to know your students, the easier it will be to make decisions about how to relate to them. (tep.uoregon.edu)

Resourceful Provider Role

American psychologist Abraham Maslow first introduced his hierarchy of needs theory in his 1943 article "A Theory of Human Motivation." The theory suggests that people are motivated to fulfill certain basic needs such as food, water, sleep, and safety before fulfilling more complex needs such as love, friendship, and personal esteem. The cold, hard fact is that we will always have some adolescent students whose basic needs are not being met at home; the percentage of these students in our programs will vary from school to school, year to year, and class to class. How can we expect students in such situations to "leave your baggage at the door, come in and make music!" if they have not eaten or slept in days? Or if finding basic clothing to wear is severely problematic? If they are living in their car with their family? Although we will not be able to fix all problems for our adolescent music students, it is admirable to make strides wherever possible. This section of chapter 2 addresses areas where we can potentially support students who are struggling and provide them with some of what they need to be able to engage in and enjoy what we are learning in our music classes.

In the school where I taught middle school choir, my students were at the lower socioeconomic end of our school district. The student population in my choral program was a mixed bag, with students coming from wealthy families moving into that side of the district, middle-class families, and low-income families. As a result, decisions with regard to concert dress, field trips, activities, and so forth began with consideration for the students whose families struggled. I wanted to make sure that everyone had a chance to be involved, regardless of their family's financial picture. For example, when field trip opportunities arose, I would solicit community businesses and individuals to sponsor students who were unable to pay for a trip (this was before the days of websites such as DonorsChoose. org). With regard to required concert dress, I kept concert attire simple and chose items that were easily attainable—white dressy shirt, black pants or skirt, and black socks or tights and shoes. I did not care about exact items that students wore (such as pants vs. skirt) other than it had to be dressy white above the waist and dressy black below the waist. Every time the seasons changed I emailed my colleagues with a list of concert clothing items, and many would donate requested pieces as they switched over seasonal wardrobes or as their children outgrew relevent items; these were housed in my classroom for anyone to borrow. When I had choir-logo shirts created (shirts for fun, not for performances), I raised the price of the hooded sweatshirt a couple of dollars—this was the most expensive of shirt choices, so students who chose this item typically did not come from families struggling with finances—and used these extra dollars to provide a choir t-shirt free of charge to any student who wanted one but could not afford one.

During interviews with the contributing middle school music teachers, I was impressed and inspired by the "above and beyond" efforts made by several of the teachers to additionally provide for their students in inventive and thoughtful ways. I would like to share a few of the efforts put forth by Bethany (general music), James (choir), and Sean (choir).

Bethany

When Bethany began teaching at her middle school, it was a very "bare bones" situation. She was hired to teach general music, but had no materials or instruments other than a piano. Unfortuately, enrollment has dropped over recent years at Bethany's school, but she was able to take advantage of the situation to enrich the general music program and creatively provide more musical opportunities for her students.

> Our school has the opposite problem from other schools and this is where I'm lucky because we have tons of empty rooms. So I just sneak rooms for myself, like, "This is my keyboard lab. This is my guitar lab. This is my storage room." We have space to do that, which is really awesome. I don't have to worry about that aspect at all.

In addition, Bethany is quite resourceful at securing classroom furniture or equipment that she needs from within and outside of her school.

> *Desks:* I have desks—the kinds of desks you can put stuff in, without chairs attached. I went around the building and purposely sought out those desks so I can use them in all sorts of different ways.
>
> *White board:* I put up my own white board. I bought shower board at Home Depot and put that up myself with some double-stick tape.
>
> *Projector:* I have a projector that I got through DonorsChoose.org. That's a website for teachers where you can describe what you would like for your classroom (I think it has to be less than $1,000 or something) and then people go to the website and donate—like random people—or you can just tell all of your friends about it and all of your friends can go to your site and donate $10 here or $15 there. When you meet your goal for that project, the site buys the stuff for you and sends it to you and it's yours! It's pretty awesome. It is only for smaller stuff, though, so we couldn't use it to build up our keyboard lab because then we'd only get one keyboard at a time— kind of slow—but I used it to get my projector, which is really great and it is helpful to have that.
>
> *Guitars:* I try to find sites, such as www.littlekidsrock.org[2]. It's a non-profit organization that trains teachers—not just music teachers, but any teachers—how to implement guitars into your classroom, as well as raise the money to get enough guitars for your school. The only requirement is that you have to already know how to play the guitar. As a result, you basically get to teach acoustic guitars in

your classroom for free. They also have drum sets and keyboards and other instruments too. So when I find a program like that, I incorporate it into what I'm already doing with the students.

James

James is very thoughtful in his efforts to show support for his middle school students. For example, When James attends choral festival or takes his students on a trip, he makes sure that everyone has a lunch to eat, especially as a large number of his students are part of the free and reduced lunch program.

> When we go on a trip and we're going to be gone for lunch, I give my class list to our lunch ladies and they will go through and pull out the 30 or 50 kids that are on free lunch or reduced lunch. And I'll say, "I want a sack lunch for every single one of those kids and the ones that it costs fifty cents for a lunch, charge my account." And so, when we go on trips and they can't pack lunches, I have three boxes full of sack lunches and can say to the free and reduced lunch students, "Don't worry. I've taken care of you." Some of those kids will pack their own lunch, anyway, so I've got extra lunches left over for those who forgot or whatever, and they're hungry. Here you go.

James also maintains a clothing closet in his choir room from which students or parents may purchase items to wear for the concerts at cost price.

> I have friends at Goodwill and I tell them, "Will you please set aside every black skirt you find and any black shoes?" I will get a couple of trash sacks full of black skirts and black shoes and they cost me a dollar or two dollars apiece. So it will cost only $50 or $100 and I have a boatload of stuff. I've got them hanging up in my closet and I will tell parents, "Here's what it cost for this skirt and here's what it cost for these pants. . . . If you have any problems with paying that amount, you talk to me and it's free to you." We also have people that donate clothes to us, including choir shirts that their students no longer need because they've moved to the high school. I'm trying to be sensitive to families' needs and make things available. And I tell my students, "Look, I was a hand-me-down family. My clothes were given to me by someone else when I was growing up." So we talk about that. "And some of your parents are out of work and you cannot afford these things. Please come talk to me. I will find a way to help you out. That's our family, that's how we clothe our kids, that's the way we function."

Sean

The Durham School of the Arts (DSA) is part of the Durham Public School District in Durham, North Carolina. And, although an arts magnet school, it is not a private school; students apply and are admitted based on a competitive lottery system and come from every corner of the entire school district. As a result, the population of the DSA is very diverse in many ways. Several students in the choral program at the DSA come from families who severely struggle socioeconomically. In response, Sean and his choral colleague, Amy Davis, provide food for these students every Monday morning, paid for with their own money. These teachers take turns each weekend picking up extra groceries that they discreetly have available to specific students, including granola bars, fruit, jars of peanut butter, and bread.

> SEAN: Students can (and do) come to us throughout the week asking to "go downstairs" (if they are with me in the upstairs room) or "go to the Chorus Closet" (if they are in the downstairs room). This, essentially, is code for, I need some food, and may I please go get some? This allows us to nod or provide them with an "errand" that helps mask what they are doing. When this happens, they tend to stay there for about 5 five minutes and eat the food before returning to their chorus class.

When approaching a long break from school, such as winter break, Sean and Amy compile a small bundle of food for these students to take with them when they leave that last day of school. They package everything in a DSA choir backpack—something that is commonly seen around the school by all students who use these backpacks to carry gym clothes, school supplies and books, or various odds and ends—so this act is truly carried out in an incredibly discreet fashion.

It is not uncommon for adolescent music students to struggle a bit during tumultuous times of development and growth, especially as everything is out of their control. As minors, they can also struggle as victims of circumstance if their family is experiencing some difficulty. However, by supporting our students through that first level of survival needs—even in small ways—we will help them to establish a bit of stable ground when in school, upon which they can build their musical knowledge and enrich their musical experiences.

Our work as music teachers is multifaceted, from the settings in which we teach to the goals we establish, to the roles that we play. All of these elements, in combination with our individual stories and life experiences, guarantee a complex and interesting ride for all who are up to the challenge. Teaching music to adolescents is not for the faint of heart, but it can be largely rewarding and a great deal of fun.

☹ AND ☺ EXPERIENCES WITH TEACHING ADOLESCENT MUSICIANS

It is so important to keep in mind that every age group has both positive and less positive characteristics. For me, adolescents are funny, quirky, brave, guarded, loyal, caring, empathetic, wicked, vicious, and occasionally a bit smelly. During our conversations, the contributing music teachers shared notable aspects of teaching adolescent musicians, ultimately compiling two delightful lists that are very representative of what it is like to work with an adolescent music population, *regardless of teaching setting*. I hesitate to say that these are "pro" and "con" lists, as I do not like the idea of there being "cons" when working with any age group. Rather, I like to think of these sorts of descriptors as challenges—hence, my use of the smiling or frowning icons. Let's say that this guy ☹ represents things that are more challenging about working with adolescent music students; oppositely, ☺ represents things that are really enjoyable about working with adolescent music students.

☹

- I know that it's part of the age because they haven't had that brain growth yet, but their inability to logically deduce anything is challenging.
- Their ability to only half-hear what you say and then twist it into something that's completely the opposite of what you said. They twist words very easily and that drives me crazy.
- The attention spans at times, especially this age group. I find that kids, more and more because of video games or computers, do not read facial expressions very well. And I'm finding that frustrating.
- They never shut up. *(laughs)* That's not entirely true. You can get them focused, but they don't know when to turn off that energy off when the time to focus arrives.
- There is a lot of drama *(chuckles)* going on with them too, you know, emotionally, physically, whatever it happens to be that day.
- Middle school does have that reputation of teasing and bullying issues. You know, kids are mean. Even with kids at our school, where the school's mission is similar to my classroom mission, there are still icky things

that happen and icky things that kids say. Today a boy came into my class crying because another boy was jealous of his skinny jeans so he put them in the toilet during dance class. It's little things that make you wonder—what? Why? How is that even possible?

- I'm definitely aware that the emotions are less predictable.
- There are those kids whose parents are forcing them to be in orchestra so their attitude reflects that, which can bring down the group dynamic.
- The only part of dealing with the kids that I don't like is their parents. I get so upset when I talk to a parent and they've never been to a concert, and I just cry for them sometimes because they have no idea that this gift that their child has even exists. So many times I want to take these kids home and just raise them and nurture them, but I can't.
- I don't like the bullying that I see in middle school. It makes me sad.
- The smell. That's probably really the only thing that I would change. I would give them all deodorant and teach them how to use it if I could! *(laughing)* That's probably one of the worst parts of the job—if not, *the* worst part of the job. A lot of what I do involves close physical proximity with my kids. Even some amount of touch—holding hands, tapping a rhythm on the upper back, and so forth, and I *really* have to work to not show my disgust on my face when I do that. And you know, I *absolutely* will not allow that to happen because I don't ever want that child to think that I'm repulsed by them—even if I am. Yeah, that's the hardest part.
- Parents who think that their kids can do no wrong. For the most part, parents are pretty reasonable. But there are some parents who hear a story from their child and it's only a partial truth. So I get angry phone calls, or angry parents, who haven't stopped to hear the other side of an issue. I don't take that very well. I'm very patient and let parents just kind of vent and express themselves. Then I say, "Let me bring some other truths to this." And usually we come to a better sense of what's going on. So that can be hard.
- Being underfunded is not fun. I remember our former band teacher saying, "Our music program is expected, but not supported."
- The biggest thing that I don't enjoy is that the kids are given very few choices of what they can do at a very young age. If you're in sixth grade you have to decide if you're going to be a music student for years to come—and if you choose music, you do not have any other options such as foreign language, art, shop, and so forth. That puts a lot of pressure on the kids and their parents when they're in fifth grade and trying to make decisions. At this age, participation in music is an experiment; this is just supposed to be a fun introduction into music. Meanwhile,

the parents are saying, "Well, you know we have to think about college." You're so far away from college and I just want your child to be able to experience music. I'm having a lot of personal struggle with this aspect of teaching middle school.

- They are at that age where they are just *fickle* about everything. They can't decide what they want. One day they love this and the next day they hate it. That kind of stuff is annoying because I do try to create lessons that they are going to be engaged in. So if they're all talking about keyboards, then I'll say, "We're all going to go to the keyboards next." And they start working on that and then they are like, "We hate keyboards!"

- The one thing that does weigh on my patience at times with middle school is the whole issue of peer conformity. I know that it's just something so inherent to the age, and it probably has always been this way. But it sometimes seems like you're combating the whole issue of conformity. What that means for students is a lack of willingness to step into an artistic frame of mind and go forward and take a risk and sing alone or do something like that in fear of what their peers would say.

- When parents' prior learning experiences haven't really helped the student develop a comfort for curiosity, comfort, compassion, or even creativity. I dislike feeling as though I have to help steer students properly when they don't come equipped with a wheel for maneuvering their "vehicle" toward the future. I guess we could call this wheel "understanding" or "awareness," and it relies on four tires, which I would call discipline, dedication, decency, and the ability to dream. Trying to rebuild a vehicle that comes damaged at the factory makes our jobs an awful lot harder. I've seen a lot of children with an awful lot of baggage in the public sector and it hurts us all as a society, as a public, and as an ensemble. And yeah, it hurts me personally to know that kids are mistreated or unloved or dismissed—they're just kids. I just can't stand that idea; kids are just kids.

☺

- Their minds are like sponges. They absorb *so* much on a day-to-day, hour-to-hour basis. It amazes me.
- I enjoy that you get to shape and mold their first times of starting an instrument, something they are always going to remember.
- I like their personalities.
- For the most part they are eager to try things. (By the time they get to high school they have pretty much made up their minds on what they want to listen to, who they want to listen to, and what advice they want.)

- They have such strong imaginations and they use their imaginations in humorous ways.
- I like that they're still kids but they're trying to be adults, so there are those moments where they're really naïve and cute and excited about things—even the kids that look like they're eighteen and have a beard—they can get excited. I really like that about them. And I like that they are still insecure because it's a little bit more of a challenge to get them to *try* things. Like I think it's my job to trick them into trying things and then liking them. I always feel successful when they're like, "I'm not going to do this," and then in the end they love it! I really like that challenge!
- The transformative or transcending power of music helps kids by elevating their way of thinking, not *just* enjoying it. And I enjoy the feeling that we're giving them something that will last a lifetime in terms of their appreciation for art, as well as a vehicle to develop other areas of their life.
- I enjoy their naiveté, their sensibility, and their inclination to learn new things without a lot of ingrained prejudice that older youths tend to exhibit.
- I enjoy their personality and their level of awkwardness.
- They let me experiment with them. Sometimes I am really up-front with them and say, "We're going to try this and see how this goes." And they're totally fine with it and they never complain about it. When they do complain about it, it lasts for five minutes at most and they're already onto another thought—whereas high schoolers' complaints will last for a whole week! *(laughs)*
- Their minds are kind of like squirrels, you know? They're on the nut and then they're at the tree and then they're like, "Oh my God, dog! I need to run!" You know? *(laughs)* So I really appreciate that about teaching them.
- I like to watch the way that they interact with each other. I think as an adult, no matter what career you are in, you have to find something to enjoy on a daily basis. And just standing in the hallways and watching them is a good moment for me. If you stand in the middle school hallway you hear hysterical things and funny conversations about things that are important to them at their age. You can reminisce: "Oh yeah, that's how I was in middle school." *(chuckles)*
- They're so moldable, in their way. And so *not* moldable in a way, you know what I mean? There are some things that you can really impress upon them, and there are other things that you'll just have to let go.
- They are fun, goofy, aloof, and willing to please.

- They need lots of guidance.
- They are learning, growing, and changing at an incredible rate. I think the physical, emotional, and social change they experience through middle school is much greater than that of high school.
- They have a lot of energy and if you can focus their attention, it can be a lot of fun. But if it's unfocused, then it's not so much fun.
- Middle schoolers are at the age where they want to be treated like young adults. And there are moments where they are just that. And those are really neat times of conversations and experiences.
- There's never a day that's the same. You know, there's always something new. There are a lot of quick developments. I'm still trying to figure out how to help guys go from unchanged voice to changed voice and take them through the process. And help them feel secure about themselves while going through that process.
- They can do amazing musical things that people don't expect. One of my pet peeves is when people say, "Well they're just middle schoolers. You can't expect them to do that." And they're like, "Yes we can."
- They can do more than people think, and they can still be kids and can have a lot of fun.
- Their sense of humor.
- I love that they wear their heart on their sleeve. They are just so ridiculously honest sometimes.
- I love that they can be a different person from one day to the next and when they appreciate something, they *really* appreciate it. And when they don't like something, they tell you! And they ask very frank questions that sometimes are difficult to answer, but they appreciate my honesty right back. So, in some ways, it's a little selfish of me because I get *so much* back from them, too. You know, I learn things from them and I get so much *love* from them, that it just comes full-circle and makes the whole thing worthwhile on a whole other level for me.
- What don't I enjoy?! I enjoy watching them experience the world for the first time. Elementary is very handholding. But middle school is where they start experiencing things on their own.
- I love watching them become young adults. When they leave me in eighth grade and there's this big shift—especially at the end-of-the-year show—there's a big shift and seeing them change and become young adults because they have complete creative control. And so, I always tell them right before the show, "Look Baby B's, it's time for you to fly. I've given you the tools and I've taught you and now it's time for you to show me what you know." And they do.

- I love their curiosity.
- I love their emotions. I love when they try to be tough, because it makes me laugh. But I love how they are experiencing all these things for the first time and we get to be part of that.
- I think my favorite thing is their limitless potential. I think a lot of directors don't see it that way and say things like, "Oh, they're middle school kids so there's no way they could do this, or perform here." Their potential really is limitless.
- I enjoy being part of the maturation of the student musician as well as the young adult. I'm one of the few teachers in the building that has them for three years, sometimes four years, depending on what feeder they go to. And it's exciting to see them mature as a responsible young adult as well as a musician.
- I love their energy and their enthusiasm.
- There's really nothing I don't like about my kids. Even when they're trying to discover hygiene and come in smelling like they just sprayed for bugs or they come in like they just came out of a garbage can.
- They're a little more independent but at the same time their minds are like a sponge so they're absorbing everything around them.
- Their enthusiasm. They're like little open books—most of them. And very willing to learn, very *excited* about learning. I enjoy getting them to do things they don't normally think they can do. Too many teachers, they don't think a middle school kid can do anything. They just think that this is some sort of transitional period—which it is, but you can still accomplish great things with them.
- At times their sense of humor can be hilarious—*accidentally*. They can say some of the dumbest things you've ever heard that are just *hilarious*.
- Mostly their enthusiasm.
- I love that I get to watch them develop, not just as musicians, but also as thinkers.
- The absolute exuberance for everything they do, especially if they're excited about it.

DIGEST

As chapter 1 focused on the adolescent music student, in this chapter we have focused on the middle-level music educator. Much of this chapter involves contemplation on individual approaches to teaching adolescent music students to encourage and deepen our thinking about our own teaching beliefs and practices, as well as to help us reflect upon the stories that have contributed (and may still contribute) to our work. You are encouraged to go forth and engage a fellow music teacher or two in this process of self-examination and reflection. Sometimes the act of discussing and comparing stories and beliefs with another person provides a greater opportunity to examine current understandings of one's work and roles as a current or future music educator.

CHAPTER 3

Cultivating Music Classroom Climate

You just gotta ignite the light
And let it shine
Just own the night
Like the Fourth of July

>   Katy Perry, *Firework* (*Perry, et. al, 2010*)

I'm beautiful in my way
'Cause God makes no mistakes
I'm on the right track, baby,
I was born this way

>   Lady Gaga, *Born This Way* (*Germanotta & Laursen, 2011*)

Successful music teachers tend to share similar aspirations for their adolescent students. These aims commonly include fostering students' musical independence and musicianship as well as empowering students during their musical development. With these two educational objectives in mind, this chapter addresses pertinent structural elements of successful middle-level music classrooms, such as acknowledgment of student diversity and maintaining the music classroom a safe place. In the next chapter, I will extend this discussion with a focus on the importance of classroom structure and matters of classroom management and discipline.

ACKNOWLEDGING STUDENT DIVERSITY

> Life is short; therefore I shall be a crusader in the struggle against ignorance and fear, beginning with myself. (Dorothy Vickers-Shelley [*Lafond, 2015*])

As music educators, we are expected to approach our teaching positions with an open mind as well as intentions of maintaining a safe place for all music students. However, this is problematic because music educators are rarely provided opportunities to contemplate and discuss how they feel about working with students of all shapes, sizes, colors, and orientations. Professor Joan Wink discussed her own process of self-discovery in her essay "Finding the Freedom to Teach and Learn, and Live," during which she realized her great biases toward certain groups of people as a result of her upbringing.

> When I left home to attend college, I met my future husband. I remember our initial conversation because he told me several things about himself that bothered me. I remember the discomfort I felt when I learned he was from Iowa. I was from South Dakota, and you know how *those people from Iowa* are. He added to my anguish when he said that he was from a farm. I was from a ranch, and you know how *those farmers* are. He further told me that his family belonged to the Farmers' Union. Horrors! My family belonged to the Farm Bureau, and you know how *those Farmers' Union people* are. I didn't ask any more questions because I was afraid of what he might say about his home culture. However, I very clearly remember wondering what his politics and religion were. You know how *those Democrats* and *Catholics* are! (Wink 2001, 209; emphasis in original)

Every adolescent music student deserves our respect, but music teachers are human and maintain assumptions and opinions about others based on a multitude of experiences and personal knowledge gained in their lifetimes. In the book *Is Everyone Really Equal? An Introduction to Key Concepts in Social Justice Education,* authors Özlem Sensoy and Robin DiAngelo discuss work by educational scholar James Banks, who made significant contributions to the idea that personal knowledge is socially constructed. So, in connection with our current conversation, it can be implied from Banks's work that, as music educators, we are who we are—wonderfulness, warts, and all—because of how our life experiences have been influenced by personal and cultural knowledge, popular knowledge, mainstream academic knowledge, school knowledge, and transformative academic knowledge. Here are Banks's five types of knowledge in more detail:

> *Personal and cultural knowledge* refers to the explanations and interpretations people acquire from their personal experiences in their homes, with their family and community cultures. This type of knowledge is based on how people were

socialized within their family. Personal and cultural knowledge is transferred both explicitly, such as direct lessons taught by family members on what constitutes politeness (e.g., "make eye contact with your elders"), as well as implicitly through messages such as what isn't talked about (e.g., race or money).

Popular knowledge refers to the facts, beliefs, and various character and plot types that are institutionalized within television, movies, and other forms of mass-mediated popular culture. Popular knowledge disseminates ideologies both implicitly and explicitly. Concepts such as the ideal family, normal relationships, and which kinds of neighborhoods are dangerous are all standardized through ongoing representations in popular culture. Because popular knowledge is widely shared, it serves as a common vocabulary and reference point. For instance, you might remember where you were when you heard about the death of Michael Jackson or what you were doing the day Prince William and Kate Middleton got married. If you asked about these events, many people would know what you were referring to and be able to say where they were too.

Mainstream academic knowledge refers to the concepts, paradigms, theories, and explanations that make up the traditional and established canon in the behavioral and social sciences. This type of knowledge is based on the belief that there is an objective truth and that with the right procedures and methods it is possible to attain this truth. Thus mainstream academic knowledge is seen as universal and applicable across all cultures. For example, many university-level courses teach theories that explain the psychological, physical, and intellectual development of children as a cohesive group. This development is said to occur through predictable stages that can be named, studied, and applied to all children, regardless of socioeconomic status, race, or gender identity.

School knowledge refers to the facts and concepts presented in textbooks, teachers' guides, and other aspects of the formal curriculum designed for use in schools. School knowledge also refers to teachers' interpretations of that knowledge. A critical component of school knowledge is not only what *is* taught, both explicitly and implicitly, but also what *is not* taught. School knowledge can also be thought of as *canonized knowledge* (or the *canon*). Canonized knowledge is knowledge that has been approved or officially sanctioned by the state, for example, through textbooks or on standardized tests. Once knowledge is canonized, it is presented as the objective truth. For example, many students are socialized to not question the textbook, but rather to accept it uncritically. Questioning school knowledge is penalized in concrete ways (grades, test scores, tracking, and reprimand) that have deep and lasting consequences for participation in society.

Transformative academic knowledge refers to the concepts and explanations that challenge mainstream academic knowledge and that expand the canon. Transformative academic knowledge questions the idea that knowledge can ever be outside of human interest, perspectives, and values. Proponents of transformative academic knowledge assume that knowledge is not neutral and that it reflects the social hierarchies of a given society. They believe that a key purpose of conceptualizing knowledge in this way is to make society more just. Transformative academic knowledge is knowledge that challenges the traditional canon. This form of knowledge recognizes that the social groups we belong to (such as race, class, and gender) necessarily shape our frame of reference and give us a particular—not a universal—perspective. Therefore, each of us has insight into some dimensions of social life but has limited understanding in others. (Sensoy and DiAngelo 2012, 8–10; emphasis in original)

As a result of influences from these five types of knowledge, "we can't help but have pre-conceived notions—prejudices—about other people based on their social groups" (ibid., 29). Both prejudice and discrimination are also discussed at length in *Is Everyone Really Equal?* and deserve mention here in our conversation. Here are three salient passages from this book:

Prejudice is learned prejudgment toward social others and refers to *internal* thoughts, feelings, attitudes, and assumptions based on the groups to which they belong. These prejudices can be either positive or negative. However, they are always unfair, because they are not earned by the individual but granted or imposed based on ideas about the *group* that the individual belongs to. (ibid., 31; emphasis in original)

How we *think* about groups of people determines how we *act* toward them. Discrimination occurs when we *act* on our prejudices. Our prejudice toward others guides our thoughts, organizes our values, and influences our actions. These prejudgments, when left unexamined, necessarily shape our behaviors. Once we act on our prejudices, we are *discriminating*. Acts of discrimination can include ignoring, avoiding, excluding, ridicule, jokes, slander, threats, and violence. (ibid., 32; emphasis in original)

If we all have our prejudices, can we avoid discriminating? Without conscious effort, this is highly unlikely; because prejudice informs how we *view* others, it necessarily informs how we *act* toward others. This action may be subtle—as subtle as avoidance and disinterest. But this lack of interest is not accidental or benign; it is socialized and results in not developing relationships. However, while we can't avoid prejudice, we can work to recognize our prejudices and gain new information and ways of thinking that will inform more just actions. (ibid., 34; emphasis in original)

Music educators, whether in music teacher preparation programs or in active teaching positions, are rarely afforded the opportunity to contemplate prejudice and discrimination. Without opportunities to recognize our prejudices, how can we be truly prepared to work with a diverse population and avoid being discriminatory?

Psychologist Dorothy Riddle developed a scale to measure the degree to which a person is or is not homophobic, called "Attitudes Towards Difference: The Riddle Scale," often referenced as "The Riddle Scale" or the "Riddle Homophobia Scale." She constructed it as a continuum with repulsion at one end, nurturance at the opposite end, and additional attitudes in-between (see Figure 3.1).

As you read the definitions of the components of The Riddle Scale below, consider *all* potential areas of diversity within your music classes (e.g., special needs, cognitive ability, English as a second language, musical talent, rural or urban, sexual orientation, race, culture, socioeconomic status, religious beliefs). Where do you feel comfortable on this continuum with regard to various groups of adolescent music students (and colleagues)? Depending upon where you "land" when considering different aspects of diversity, what are the implications for your teaching or interactions with students (or colleagues)?

> *Repulsion*—People who are different are strange, sick, crazy, and aversive. Anything that will change them to be more normal or part of mainstream is justifiable. Homosexuality is seen as a "crime against nature."
>
> *Pity*—People who are different are somehow born that way and that is pitiful. Being different is definitely immature and less preferred. To help those poor individuals, one should reinforce normal behaviors. Heterosexual chauvinism.
>
> *Tolerance*—Being different is just a phase of development that most people go through and most people "grow out of." Thus they should be protected and tolerated as one does a child who is still learning. Gays and lesbians should not be given positions of authority because they are still working through adolescent behaviors.
>
> *Acceptance*—Implies that one needs to make accommodations for another's differences and does not acknowledge that another's identity may be of the same value as one's own. Denies some of the social and legal realities; ignores the pain of invisibility and stress of "closet behavior."

Repulsion * Pity * Tolerance * Acceptance *

Figure 3.1 Attitudes Towards Difference: The Riddle Scale.

Support—Works to safeguard the rights of those who are different. Such people might be uncomfortable themselves, but they are aware of the climate and irrational unfairness in our society.

Admiration—Acknowledges that being different in our society takes strength. Such people are willing to truly look at themselves and work on their own personal biases.

Appreciation—values diversity of people and is willing to confront insensitive attitudes in themselves and others.

Nurturance—Assumes the differences in people are indispensable in society. They view differences with genuine affection and delight and are willing to be advocates of those differences. (Riddle, 1994, 34–35)

The words "tolerance" and "acceptance" are often used in conversations about diversity. However, according to The Riddle Scale there are differences between tolerating and/or accepting diversity and embracing diversity through nurturance. Consider the following: Religious tolerance means accepting and respecting the right of different religions to exist. But that is different from finding value in those differences or of feeling enriched by knowing people of different faiths. Also, many music teachers consider "inclusion" to mean tolerating or accepting the presence of cognitively or musically limited students, as required by law. But tolerating music students does not signify a willingness to advocate for those differences.

In adolescent music classes, "diversity" can mean different things and, as a result, impact a music class in varied ways: different cultural backgrounds can enrich the group; different musical levels can affect performance goals; and the presence of disruptive, behaviorally disordered or emotionally impaired students can affect the learning of the group. As humans and music teachers, we may find ourselves more receptive to some types of diversity than others in our music classes. What is important is that we recognize how we view our music students—whether as "a problem," "a

Support * Admiration * Appreciation * Nurturance

Figure 3.1 Continued.

great resource," or "a community service project"—and find ways to show respect to all adolescent students operating and interacting in our music classes.

It is not uncommon for music educators to approach student diversity with a plan to treat all adolescents the same. However, claiming to be "colorblind" with the promise that everyone will be treated the same is problematic. As Wendy Goodman wrote in *Living (and Teaching) in an Unjust World*, "There is a tendency to assume that we can achieve equality by ignoring differences and treating all children as if they are the same. Sometimes, in the face of inequality, we deny its very existence" (Goodman 2001, 4). Dr. Gloria Ladson-Billings also addressed teacher claims of colorblindness in her book *The Dreamkeepers: Successful Teachers of African American Children*, bringing attention to equality versus sameness:

> Given the significance of race and color in American society, it is impossible to believe that a classroom teacher does not notice the race and ethnicity of the children she is teaching. Further, by claiming not to notice, the teacher is saying that she is dismissing one of the most salient features of the child's identity and that she does not account for it in her curricular planning and instruction. Saying we are aware of students' race and ethnic background is not the same as saying we treat students inequitably. The passion for equality in the American ethos has many teachers (and others) equating equality with sameness. (Ladson-Billings 2009, 36)

Goodman's and Ladson-Billing's words are critical and apply to all considerations of student diversity, not just race. When speaking with middle school music teachers for this book, I asked them how matters of diversity impacted their music classrooms—purposefully leaving the word "diversity" open for their individual interpretations. Responses pertained specifically to racial and ethnic diversity, socioeconomic diversity, and diversity of student ability. Contemplation of these areas within our own music classes provides us a starting point for consideration of many other forms of diversity within specific music student populations. This need not be daunting and, in fact, it can be exhilarating. Sean (choir) shared, "My classes are actually, truly diverse. There's no token anything. It's such a palate, truly, which to me is so wonderful and beautiful and it's natural too." James (choir) embraced the diversity of his students as well:

> I had a girl in class two years ago who was from Serbia and it just so happened she lived two houses down from me. I said, "Can I come talk to your mom about this song?" And I went over to my neighbor's house and we sat down for an hour and she told me all about Serbia and her religious traditions and so forth. Learning about each other is just great! If we can do songs from a student's culture, they can provide an authenticity that would not necessarily be present if they weren't in our class.

Acknowledging student diversity, however, does not mean that we view our individual students as walking labels. Instead of "Chad is physically disabled," it is more constructive to frame thinking as, "Chad is a student who has a physical disability." Labeling has been especially problematic for students who identify as lesbian, gay, bisexual, transgender, or queer (LGBTQ), for a student who comes out to peers often becomes "the gay kid" and loses other aspects of identity. The following firsthand account is from an interview with Brett, an undergraduate music education student who self-identifies as gay:

> BRETT: I mean I'm not the type that as soon as you meet me I say *(speaking very quickly)*, "Hi I'm Brett. By the way, I'm gay." *(slowing speech again)* Like ... it's ... I don't think it's a defining factor of who I am as a person. I mean it makes up part of who I am but it's definitely not *who* I am. So I don't think it's the absolute first thing you should know about me. I am much more wanting them to get me to know me as a *person* and my *personality* and then, "Oh ... he just so happens to be gay." Because I hate being introduced as, "This is my gay friend, Brett." No ... I'm your *friend*, Brett, who *happens* to be gay.
>
> BRIDGET: Do people introduce you that way?
>
> BRETT: Yeah. I have been introduced that way. And I don't know if it's true, but in *my* mind I think it takes away from the friendship. Like, if I wasn't gay, would we be friends? Why do I have you be your *gay* friend?
>
> BRIDGET: You're like the token.

BRETT: Yeah! Am I like the token gay here? *(both laughing)* Am I meeting your status quo? *(both laughing more)* Yeah. It's just . . . I don't want to be labeled as just "gay." There's *so* much more to me—at least *I* think—than my sexuality.

Brett's remarks align with writings by Paula Kluth and Kevin P. Colleary, who addressed the labeling of students as a move away from preserving student dignity in "'Talking about Inclusion Like It's for Everyone': Sexual Diversity and the Inclusive Schooling Movement":

> Although no teacher would admit to intentionally treating students without respect, and every teacher would claim to value the preservation of student dignity, teachers can easily reduce a student, especially a student questioning his or her own sexuality, to emotional rubble with a word, a glance, or the silence provoked by fear or uncertainty. (Kluth and Colleary 2002, 110)

Kluth and Colleary's comments specifically pertain to students who self-identify as LGBTQ, but their message of respect and valuing multiple aspects of a student can be applied to all categories of student diversity.

Following the acknowledgment of our adolescent music students as a group of diverse individuals, we must take the next step toward joining our diverse student population together as one whole entity of a music class or ensemble. In my mind, a visual representation of this objective is that of a larger image composed of hundreds of smaller images. For example, I have seen a poster that, from far away, is a picture of Yoda from the *Star Wars* movies. However, up close, Yoda is actualized by special placement of hundreds of individual scenes taken from the *Star Wars* movies. Without just one of those tiny images, the larger picture of Yoda would be distorted. So, our endeavors as music educators are more realistically obtained if we recognize the unique role that each adolescent student plays in the larger picture of a music class or ensemble. Without recognition of each person, the larger picture is flawed.

Some of the middle school music teachers interviewed for this book discussed their work toward a unified, diverse middle school classroom. "Making music together is an extraordinary way to unite people of different backgrounds. We have diversity, which is great, but we're all working together to produce something that actually transcends all of us. And adolescents as young as sixth grade can understand that" (David, choir and guitar). Michelle (choir) had students from across the entire socioeconomic spectrum, from very poor, homeless students to incredibly wealthy students. Nonetheless, she held fast to her belief that, when singing in a middle school choir, socioeconomic differences between her students were hardly apparent.

> MICHELLE: I know this is going to sound really cliché, but one of the benefits that we have in our subject matter is that anyone can sing. It doesn't matter how poor you are, how rich you are—anyone can sing. And when you have all those kids standing up there at the concert, wearing the same thing, singing the same thing, no one looks at them and says, "Wow. You can really tell who the poor kids are." Or "Wow, you can see the rich kids." Because you can't. They're all speaking the same thing. They're all up on that stage with everyone else, participating, feeling proud and that really makes a difference.

Jason (band) maintained high expectations from every one of his band students, despite varying physical abilities, because these students contributed to the collective whole.

> JASON: We've had some students where, given a specific task, they weren't able to do it because of a specific modification—whether it be a physical or a health-related thing. But I try to keep that bar up as high as I can for those students—if not equal to the others—and I think the bottom line is that they appreciate that. Just because some hurdles come to us doesn't mean that we necessarily have to lower expectations.

As discussed in the first section of this chapter, countless experiences and personal interactions have influenced who we are and our work as music educators, influencing our choices of musical literature, topics for discussion in music classes, decisions regarding worthy musical experiences for students, methods of planning, interactions with adolescent music students and colleagues (or lack thereof), and so forth. Through our choices we will, in turn, influence our adolescent music students in a variety of ways, especially in regard to the treatment of others. Our students will watch us closely, listen to what we say, and observe how we act both inside and outside of the music classroom, and then they will go forth and emulate what we model.

Thus, just as it is important that we gain an understanding of why we believe what we believe, it is important that we encourage independent thinking in our music classes and cultivate environments where students may examine why they believe what they believe—both about diverse music and musical experiences, as well as diverse people. "We must always be ready to meet and engage with others who are very different from ourselves. This is a lesson that we as adults must understand, and it is a lesson that we as teachers can share with and model for our students during their earliest years in school" (Kluth and Colleary 2002, 108)

SAFE PLACES

> SEAN (CHOIR): These students are coming into my room because they like music. But I also want them to come into my room knowing that they are safe in here and can be themselves. They can laugh, they can be goofy; they can make a mistake and learn from that. But along the way, while we're learning the music, we're kind of figuring out what to do in this world as different kinds of people.

In today's rapidly changing world, the idea of school safety is a bit scary. My first year as a teacher was the year of the Columbine High School shooting. The day after the shooting, I came to school and the students were visibly shaken by the incident; we all were. My first-hour class of seventh graders wanted to talk about it, so we did. But as a brand new, first-year teacher, I had never been trained to lead such a conversation. I did not know how to respond to their questions: "Why did that happen?" "Could this happen here?" And the most gut-wrenching one of all: "Would you protect us if someone came to hurt us?" I responded in the best ways I could, trying to give the students some sense of power in their proposed scenarios. But the bottom line was that my students were not tough teenagers in this moment. These were scared kids who lived during a time when school evacuation plans had mostly focused on the idea of escaping building fires. Since then, teachers have been trained, practiced intruder drills, talked with their students about hiding places and evacuation plans, and maintained hope to never be faced with such situations in real time.

In this book, discussion of the music classroom as a safe place and/or safe space is not about how we can protect our students and ourselves from school intruders. Rather, the intention is to discuss music classrooms as nonthreatening places where adolescent music students can escape the scrutiny (real or imagined) of others. In their research article "Safe Space: Student Perspectives on Classroom Environment," Lynn C. Holley and Sue Steiner described safe space as follows:

> A classroom climate that allows students to feel secure enough to take risks, honestly express their views, and share and explore their knowledge,

attitudes, and behaviors. Safety in this sense does not refer to physical safety. Instead, classroom safe space refers to protection from psychological or emotional harm. A safe classroom space is one in which students are able to openly express their individuality, even if it differs dramatically from the norms set by the instructor, the profession, or other students. (Holley and Steiner 2005, 50)

For a moment I would like to discuss the four key components of a safe (or unsafe) classroom space that Holley and Steiner designated via their research: instructor characteristics, peer characteristics, personal characteristics, and physical environment characteristics. Although the primary participants of their study were students in collegiate social work programs, Holley and Steiner's findings absolutely apply to our work as teachers of adolescents. They describe the same essential components necessary for fostering a music classroom environment where adolescent students can thrive and feel open to express their individuality—especially in the midst of figuring out who they are and what they believe about music (and everything else), as they navigate great physical, emotional, and cognitive growth.

The first component of a safe classroom environment concerns *instructor characteristics*. In safe spaces, instructors were described as

being nonjudgmental or unbiased; as developing ground rules for class discussion or modeling how to participate; as being comfortable with conflict or raising controversial ideas; as being respectful or supportive of others' opinions; as encouraging or requiring active participation in class; and as demonstrating caring. Relative to their representation in the sample, students of color were more likely to say that the instructor's attention to cultural issues was important in creating a safe space. (ibid., 57)

In unsafe classrooms, instructors "were critical of or chastised students; were biased, opinionated, or judgmental; and refused to consider one's opinions" (ibid.).

Peer characteristics in safe classroom spaces involved peers "practicing good discussion skills; honestly sharing their thoughts, ideas, opinions, or facts; being nonjudgmental and open to new ideas, perspectives, or experiences; and sharing a sense of community" (ibid.). Peers in unsafe spaces were "biased, judgmental, or close-minded; were apathetic about the course; and tried to please the instructor."

The third component, *personal characteristics*, pertained to how students' own behaviors contributed to an environment of safety in the classroom.

These included "be open-minded; honestly share ideas, views, and values; actively participate in discussion; be supportive of or respectful toward others; and be prepared for class" (ibid.). In unsafe classroom spaces, students acknowledged that they "did not participate; they were fearful, worried, intimidated, insecure, unconfident, or felt vulnerable; and that they did not invest in the course" (ibid.).

Physical environment characteristics involved literal details of safe and unsafe classrooms. "Students overwhelmingly indicated that seating arrangements that allowed class members to see everyone (e.g., sitting in a circle or square) contributed to the creation of such a space. Students also commonly said that an appropriate-sized room (e.g., not too large or too small for the number of students) and good lighting were important" (ibid.). Students identified row-style seating as a common characteristic of an unsafe classroom.

Now consider Holley and Steiner's findings in comparison to your own music classroom. How do you regard such components? When considering instructor characteristics and physical environment characteristics, which of those described align with your personality and/or manifest in your classroom? What are the implications of certain characteristics in your behaviors and/or classroom space? Two of the contributing components of a safe classroom were peer characteristics and personal characteristics—but these are really the responsibility of individual students, right? *Not exactly,* as our adolescent music students don't know what they don't know. Thus part of our work as music educators is to enlighten our students about the importance of being good people and supportive classroom citizens, as well as to edify them in music.

In his article "'Safe Spaces': Reflections on an Educational Metaphor," Robert Boostrom expressed concern that momentum of the idea of safe space in education would ultimately censor critical thinking in the classroom in order to avoid stress for students. In his words:

> Understood as the avoidance of stress, the "safe space" metaphor drains from classroom life every impulse toward critical reflection. It's one thing to say that students should not be laughed at for posing a question or for offering a wrong answer. It's another to say that students must never be conscious of their ignorance. It's one thing to say that students should not be belittled for a personal preference or harassed because of an unpopular opinion. It's another to say that students must never be asked why their preferences and opinions are different from those of others. It's one thing to say that students should be capable of self-revelation. It's another to say that they must always like what they see revealed. (Boostrom 1998, 406)

It is important to note that maintaining one's classroom as a safe place does not mean that discomfort, struggle, conflict, or difference of opinion are excluded from the music classroom. Safe place does not sterilize a classroom of all creative or critical thinking—"being safe is not the same as being comfortable" (Holley and Steiner 2005, 50). Rather, the goal is to foster music classroom environments where "the encouragement of open and honest communication is a goal, an atmosphere or classroom climate should be created where students feel that they are able to risk honesty with the knowledge that they will not suffer too greatly for it" (ibid., 51).

All intentions regarding safe place in this book are to promote a music classroom environment where adolescent students are not belittled, where they feel free to push the boundaries of musical thinking and performing, and where they feel empowered to be themselves—their varied, unique selves. I want music teachers to challenge adolescent critical thinking through inquiries including *why* do you think, feel, perform, and believe the ways that you do? How is your musical interpretation and thinking different from other people and why is that important within the realm of learning and experiencing music, as well as in personal development? My hope is that all honest opinions are honored and valued, whether as insight and/or important discourse in the music classroom, furthering thinking, discussion, musical interpretation, and performance practice for all adolescent musicians as well as their music teachers.

Within safe musical spaces, musicianship tends to flourish as adolescents take more artistic risks where support is received and mistakes are honored. "If they don't feel safe, they're not going to experiment or try" (James, choir). "They know it's okay to make mistakes and that's how they learn and that they're still going to be loved" (Tavia, band). "I do try to make my room *forgiving*, shall we say. Mistakes are necessary; that's how you learn" (Gretchen, strings).

> DEB (CHOIR): We understand how important and how precious it is when somebody has the guts. And I'll tell them, "I don't care if a small ferret flies out of your throat, nobody's going to laugh at you. Even if it looks darn funny if a ferret flies out of your throat, we're not laughing." And I never say *you'd* better not make fun of a kid, it's always "if somebody you are sitting next to makes *you* feel bad they are *so* out of here."

The middle school teachers spoke proudly of their music class environments and genuinely felt that students perceived their rooms as places of respect and respite from peer criticism. "My students know that this is your family. This is a safe place for you to be. This is somewhere you can express yourself. It's somewhere where you should feel comfortable being you" (Robyn, strings). "After school and in the mornings they hang out in the band room. I think that speaks volumes; this is their home away from home—not to sound too corny with that" (Jason, band). "We are prepared for safety from weather and intruders. Safe from ridicule and emotional harm. My class offers sanctuary. Sanctuary from all the other problems outside the door. We sing. We laugh. We work hard. We indulge ourselves in a break from all that is not chorus" (Jay, choir and composition). Kate (general music) promoted her classroom as a safe place for infinite possibilities:

KATE: I always say that if you're going to make a mistake, make it loudly. So whether it's in my general music classroom or in my choir, I am myself and encourage them to be themselves, whatever that means on that particular day. And to take risks. Like when we are playing the drums, I say, "There is no wrong answer. Play whatever you feel. Just play one beat, if you need to. But there it is. You put something out there. And you did it and nobody's going to argue with it. And it's there." And I love being in a music classroom because it's one of the only places where you can have that infinite number of correct answers. Where they can be successful, no matter their skill level, background—no matter who they are.

Michelle (choir) and Kate's (general music) music classrooms have been officially designated as safe places within the larger school by their school administration. Students are allowed to visit their rooms at any time of the day for a few moments to refocus themselves or if they are having an especially difficult day for whatever reason. School policies and guidelines have made this arrangement successful for both teachers and students in their buildings, and Michelle and Kate are proud to fulfill this role in their schools.

KATE: I really pride myself for this. I take a special interest in LGBTQ issues in schools, as I'm the founder of the Gay-Straight Alliance in my school, and from the get-go I've been really strict about language toward others in my room. Respect is very, very important and students don't always understand what that means. They don't understand that when they are teasing each other and calling each other names that they are still hurting each other. They've learned that they just don't do that in my room. I actually had a kid catch himself. He called another kid a faggot and he said (in *a fast, hushed, apologetic voice)*, "Oh my goodness, Ms. Tyler, I'm so sorry. I forgot that you don't like it when we say that in your room." He was like *(again, in a fast, apologetic voice)* "It will never happen again! I'm so sorry! Please don't write me up!" So, they know that there is going to be a consequence when they are in my room or in my presence. Now I wish they would translate that to other places outside of my room—especially the hallways.

In chapter 2, discussion of the music teacher as a resourceful provider included mention of Abraham Maslow and his hierarchy of needs theory. As a refresher: the theory suggests that people are motivated to fulfill certain basic needs such as food, water, sleep, and safety before fulfilling more complex needs such as love, friendship, and personal esteem. Several of the music teachers described efforts to meet some of the basic needs of their music students during the school year. Matthew (band) specifically referenced Maslow's hierarchy as a foundational piece of the safe environment of his band classroom.

> MATTHEW: I apply Maslow's hierarchy of human needs to having safety in the music classroom. With things like physical space—is it orderly with clear expectations? When students walk in, do they know what's expected of them and their behavior? Do they know something as simple as what's going to happen in the next forty minutes? The more we can do to clarify expectations and keep students engaged and on-task for the greatest amount of time, the higher you can get in the pyramid of learning. More learning can occur when the students feel like the educational environment is safe. If students walk in and nothing's been communicated, there's unstructured time ... naturally students are going to socialize because clearly they don't know what else to do. Misbehaviors occur and, as a result, and there is no learning going on. And if there is any kind of bullying, there's no learning going on. If there is physical fighting, no learning is going to occur, period. We are all the way back down to survival mode—students fear for their physical safety. So the more that we can provide a safe environment, it's only going to help increase academic achievement.

The possibility of music students not feeling safe in their music classes bothered several of the teachers. Sean (choir) spoke at length about his work to ensure that the choir classroom was a safe place for his students, especially since he had little control over spaces outside of his classroom.

SEAN: You know, I can't account for the hallways, I can't account for the cafeteria, I can't account for your math class, but in *this room* you can be who you are. You can come in here every day and know that, no matter what's happening anywhere else in your life or in this building, when you come here you can exhale and just let what will be, be. Everyone in here is going to respect your boundaries and is going to respect your right to be whatever it is you might be. Is everyone in here going to be your best friend? No. But we have established the idea that in this space it's cool to be and to feel whatever you want.

Deb's Safe Place

In Deb's (choir) classroom, Safe Place was a capitalized, formal idea that guided all interactions and allowed for a risk-free, no-pressure singing environment.

DEB: This whole concept of Safe Place is *so* integral to my classroom. That, not only when you are singing a solo, you get to be safe in here. If you answer a question, we are respectful of you. Period. And nobody gets a second chance to hurt somebody's feelings because it's not *ever* accidental if you are unkind.

The paramount role of Safe Place in Deb's choral program resulted from three stories in her musical career. The first two stories involved traumatic singing experiences where Deb was too paralyzed with fear to sing in front of others. The third story happened ten years after Deb graduated from St. Olaf and was teaching at an elementary school in Michigan before she was assigned to work with the middle school students in her district. I present the entire story here in Deb's own words. It's on the long side, but it is a powerful story and the way she tells it is significant to our understanding of how important Safe Place is to her:

DEB: I had kids sing their name in kindergarten *(Deb begins to sing-song names with the second name an echo of the first),* "Sarah, Sarah" "Ben, Ben." I had a girl in kindergarten—I'll call her Bridget—who wouldn't sing by herself. So it would be "Marcus [Marcus echoes]" "Bridget [no echo—silence]" and I didn't make a big deal of it. By the end of kindergarten the kids knew we were going to do the circle name game and nobody expected Bridget to sing. I still sang

Bridget's name and the game would go right on. First grade, same thing. Second grade, nobody expected it. Third grade, I said, "Oh man! Just humor me! Humor me! Let's take a walk down memory lane with the name game." "Marcus [Marcus echoes]" "Bridget [*very, very softly* Bridget echoes]" and the whole class went (*looking sharply to her left where Bridget sat, eyes open in amazement*). Honest to God. They were just—*she's a-live!* And I didn't make a big deal of it. I mean I kind of went (*sits up with a surprised look on her face, slightly nodding her head*) and went on. And by the end of third grade, "Marcus [Marcus echoes]" "Bridget [*very softly* Bridget echoes]" "Marvin [Marvin echoes]," and Bridget was *consistently* singing her name. Not more than that, but she would do that. The class cheered for her, they made her feel good, and I'm thinking, "God, I have got it so well together, I am like teacher extraordinaire." (I think you can sense what's coming.) No Safe Place yet—didn't know about Safe Place yet—but wanted kids to be singing. Fourth grade, "Let's do solos today! Let's do solos on 'America the Beautiful'!" I always have started out with little solos and kids have been very good about doing little solos in my space. Well, third or fourth or fifth time that year, "Who wants to do part of a line on 'America the Beautiful'?" and *whoosh!* eighteen hands went up and all of a sudden. . . . here's Bridget (*Deb bashfully and tentatively raises her hand, imitating Bridget*). "Take it away, Bridget!" And she goes . . . (*imitating Bridget, who shakes her head no and takes down her hand*). So we all went on and then a month later, two months later, "Anybody want to?. . . . okay, Marvin and Ralph and . . . Bridget would you? Would you like to?" (*imitating Bridget, shakes head no*). A couple months later, you could just see it . . . (*imitating Bridget looking interested in singing solo, subtly nodding head yes*). "Bridget?" And she said yes . . . (*imitating Bridget nodding yes*). So I'm thinking "for purple mountain majesties," you know, it's *low*, it's in a *sa-afe* range. (*dryly*) And being the master teacher, I would be one to prethink that. So we gave out our eight solos and by this point people were so used to this song it just wasn't a big deal. The first kid sings, "Oh beautiful for spacious skies," and the second kid sings, "for amber waves of grain," and I can see Bridget's just . . . (*looking down the line at her impending solo, terrified*). I mean, she's me. She's me just seeing it coming. And she starts to sing, "for purple mountain," and her voice cracks (*Deb makes a sound with her voice that resembles sliding from a higher pitch to a lower pitch*) and it was the funniest damn thing you'd ever hear. The kids laughed. *Not* to make fun of her because they were *so* excited that she was singing. They giggled because it was, it was friggin' funny! It sounded like a . . . like a . . . frog or something coming out of her throat. She burst into tears and ran out of the room. Next time in music I said, "You guys remember that darn name game?" I'm thinking, "back it up, back it up." "Marcus [Marcus echoes]" "Bridget [silence]." *She never sang another word in my class.* I lost a kid and I spent four and a half years working this kid. Oh my God. That is one of the darkest moments of *my* teaching was when I lost this kid. Clink. The concept of . . . in official capital letters: "SAFE (*mouths an expletive between words*) PLACE." And so, to this day I tell the kids why and how Safe Place got started. And they know I lost a kid and that it just still grates at me that I lost a kid.

Violations of Safe Place in Deb's classroom ranged from temporary to permanent removal from choir. In reality, no student had ever been permanently removed from choir because of such a violation, but Deb told many stories of students who had "experienced her wrath" as a result of their non–Safe Place actions or words. One specific story was about a boy who overtly shunned another student with Down Syndrome during choir. She immediately pulled the offending student into the hallway for a private conversation:

DEB: How *dare* you. This kid not only has to wake up every morning with a syndrome he sure as heck never asked for, but he has to have some *jerk* (and that's just not me to use that word), some jerk sit down and make him feel like a "retard." (*voice very soft and hissing*) H-h-how dare you. I said, "You know what? I don't want that kind of kid in my choir. You've got a really important choice to make. Because if this is really who you are, I don't want you in my choir."

Deb openly admitted that this particular situation was especially upsetting for her because of the story of her own niece who, as a special needs child, experienced a great deal of negativity from classmates as a result of her developmental disabilities. This story did have a happy ending: the student remained in choir and became a huge advocate for the choral program as well for the special needs students who participated. In fact, he began to intentionally seek out the student with Down Syndrome during class and they became genuine friends.

While I applaud the positive efforts of this particular student following this incident, I largely credit Deb for his turnaround and new perspective. Her efforts with Safe Space made a difference to students, and this concept was a major component of their experiences in choir, according to the students: "It's a great class to build your confidence and build skills without worrying that you're going be made fun of." Within Safe Place, Deb's students gained confidence to try, which allowed them to develop their musical skills. Below is a snippet of a conversation about Safe Place with one of her students (identified by a pseudonym).

> BEN: Safe Place is where you can sing in front of your peers without having to be embarrassed or anything if you *do* mess up and they won't laugh or anything. And if you're just telling Mark, "You're doing really good," she'll be like, "What are you saying?" or "Don't whisper to people" because the person will think that you're saying something bad *automatically*. They'll feel bad and then it completely ruins the safe place.
>
> BRIDGET: So if someone is singing to the group, you don't even talk to your other friend to say, "Hey, I like your new shoes," because the person in front of the room could think you were saying something mean about them.
>
> BEN: She just . . . she doesn't allow it. It's a really cool thing.

DIGEST

In this chapter, focus has remained on important structural elements of successful middle school music classrooms, including the acknowledgment of student diversity and maintaining the music classroom as a safe place for adolescent music students. When adolescent music students feel accepted and safe in their music classroom, they are more willing to try new tasks and take musical risks, especially during times of great (and often unpredictable) physical, cognitive, and emotional development. As a result, musicality and technical skills flourish and our students gain a better idea of who they are and how they interpret the musical world.

Follow-up Activities

As we consider diversity and safe place within our own music education programs, it is wise to begin with self-reflection and contemplation on the stories and experiences that have contributed to our current teaching methods and beliefs, as well as reflect on ways that we can improve and deepen our practice as music educators of adolescents. Here are a few activities to get you started.

- "Attitudes Towards Difference: The Riddle Scale"

Consider yourself in comparison to the "Attitudes Towards Difference" scale created by Dorothy Riddle. Where do you place yourself on this scale regarding various groups of adolescent music students? Colleagues? What are implications for your teaching and/or interactions with students (and/or colleagues) based on how you identify with the Riddle scale?

- *Personal culture examination*

Professor Owen van den Berg requires students to focus on personal culture for the first assignment of his undergraduate course in cultural diversity. (For further details of his classroom approach, see his chapter "Affirming Difference While Building a Nation: Teaching Diversity in Neo-Apartheid America" in the book *Living (and Teaching) in an Unjust World*). Instructions are as follows: Reflect on your own life and the way in which you have been socialized or educated into a particular culture, and attempt to describe the keystones of that personal culture.

I often have my music education undergraduate students complete van den Berg's activity and the results are fascinating. The aspects of personal culture on which students choose to focus are intriguing and quite varied. From this experience, students gain a deeper awareness of how culturally driven belief systems guide their own thinking, beliefs, and behaviors, which is valuable as they form and develop their individual music education philosophies and teaching methods.

- *Critical questioning*

Two sets of questions follow for reflection and discussion on matters of culture, identity, diversity, and difference. Music teachers are encouraged to contemplate the questions on their own, but to also engage other music educators in discussions on such matters. Through respectful conversation that includes both agreement and discourse, thinking is broadened and deepened, as are considerations of teaching practice.

The first set is from Jill Gladstein's chapter "Using Critical Questioning to Investigate Identity, Culture, and Difference," also in the book *Living (and Teaching) in an Unjust World*, in which she poses valuable questions for reflection and discussion on matters of culture, identity, and difference: (a) What is culture? (b) What is identity? (c) How do others see me in American society? (d) How are identity and culture connected? (e) What is difference? (f) How do identity, culture, and difference exist in American society?

The second set of questions focuses on diversity and comes from the book *Learning to Teach for Social Justice* by Linda Darling-Hammond, Jennifer French, and Silvia Paloma Garcia-Lopez: (a) What does diversity mean to you? (b) What are the implications of human diversity for learning and teaching and for the work of educators? (c) What are the dilemmas posed by diversity in schools? (d) How do our own backgrounds shape how we view diversity? (e) How does rhetoric about inclusion match reality in schools you have experienced as a student or a teacher?

- *Developing self-awareness*

The following exercises come from book *Is Everyone Really Equal? An Introduction to Key Concepts in Social Justice Education* (Sensoy and DiAngelo 2012).

1. Choose a song, newspaper article, textbook passage, novel, film, commercial, or other text. Identify which of the various forms of knowledge (personal/cultural knowledge, popular knowledge, school knowledge, mainstream academic knowledge, transformative knowledge) manifest in the text, and describe how. (ibid., 13)
2. Generate a list of actions (verbs) and personality attributes (characteristics) that people in various occupations perform and have.
   For example:

Teacher	Environmentalist	Librarian
Police officer	Dentist	Stay-at-home parent
Soldier	Counselor	Scientist
Farmer	Housekeeper	Car wash attendant
Musician	Music educator	

   What is the "picture in your mind" that you have of the person who holds that occupation? What gender, race, and class is that person? Does the person have a visible disability? Is she or he someone who will observe religious/holy days? If so, which ones?
   Then compare your list with others' lists. What are the implications of these "pictures in our minds" for the ways we might behave toward the person? And what are the implications of the *awareness* of these "pictures in our minds" for the ways we might behave toward the person? (ibid., 36)
3. Get a magazine and choose 10 photos of people. Swap your photos with others (so you are working with a different set). Rank the people in the photos according to each of these questions. Then try picking one question and ranking all 10 photographs for that attribute, for example, from "smartest" to "not the smartest."

a. Who's the smartest?
b. Who's the wealthiest?
c. Who's the most religious?
d. Who reads a lot?
e. Who's careful with money?
f. Who's a stay-at-home parent?
g. Who's the most likely to feel included in society?
h. Who's the most likely to feel isolated?
i. Who is the most likely to be put in charge?
j. Who is the most likely to travel freely anywhere in the world?

Now interview two people (other than those engaged in the activity with you), asking them to do what you did. What patterns do you notice in the responses? How did an awareness of your prejudices (or preconceived ideas) influence the decisions you made in response to each of the questions? (ibid., 37)

CHAPTER 4

Establishing the Framework
for Successful Music Classes

Success is a journey, not a destination. The doing is often more important than
the outcome. (Arthur Ashe [*Arthur Ashe Learning Center, 2009*])

In this chapter, we will continue to explore issues discussed in the previous
chapter regarding the development of student musical independence and
the empowerment of adolescent music students. The focus here includes the
importance of classroom structure, matters of classroom management and
discipline, interactions with students, and student engagement.

FLEXIBILITY WITHIN STRUCTURE

Because adolescents tend to feel powerless over their bodies and lives,
knowledge provides them with a sense of power. When privy to information
in music class—be it a daily agenda, diagrams and explanation of how voices
change, or even the designated time for the next fire drill—adolescents
may act more rationally and more predictably because they know what
to expect. When they understand what is coming and what is happening,
they have a semblance of control. That said, adolescents are also different
every day and there is no predicting the mood of each music class until they
walk in the door. So when melding adolescents' desire for information with
adolescents' unpredictability (be it emotional or physiological, especially
when considering the male and female changing voice), a sensible music
classroom framework is one of flexibility within a structured system. Note

that in speaking of flexibility and structure, I am promoting these ideas as pedagogical approaches and not discussing classroom management or discipline. (That conversation comes later in this chapter.)

Consider flexibility and structure as intersecting continua: one x-axis continuum and one y-axis continuum (see Graph 4.1). Music educators will plot classroom approaches differently on such a graph because we are each drawn to structure and flexibility in our own way as a result of past experiences, training, and the settings in which we teach.

Flexibility does not mean fly-by-the-seat-of-your-pants teaching, because we should always be *prepared*. However, in a flexible environment, our methods of teaching music are more contingent upon our particular students in *this* current time and place. Flexibility also provides space for fickle adolescent moods and emotions. Kate, who teaches general music, said, "I'll throw a whole lesson out the window if I start it and I see that it's just not going to go with this group that day, you know? Or I'll modify it. No two classes can ever be taught exactly the same way." In my own work with adolescent music students, I have found that music classes are much harder to facilitate on the day of a school dance, a pep assembly, before a long break, or a big societal event like Halloween—especially during the last hours of the school day. My lessons were more successful when I allowed for flexibility in my plans and anticipated student need for high-energy activities, perhaps involving small group work, kinesthetic creativity, or movement.

The contributing music teachers approached flexibility and structure in varied ways. Some were more flexible on a daily basis, such as Kate (general music): "I've learned to be so playful with them and that's the most important thing, I think. I give them structure, but I also give them room."

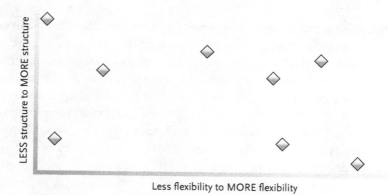

Graph 4.1 Structure vs. Flexibility.

Others, such as Bethany (general music), were more flexible from semester to semester, creating lessons and environments to specifically address the unique needs of her adolescent music students from class to class in real time, often through current events (music related and not). Tavia (band) was more middle-of-the-road with regard to structure, in that she planned long-term for her music students but remained flexible on short-term details, depending upon how her students were progressing:

TAVIA: I do try to plan at least a few months out (and have tried planning for a whole year). But I keep an open mind as I go because I might discover something that I thought was going to be a good fit—but maybe this section didn't advance as much as I thought they would and it may not be a good fit anymore. So I adjust accordingly. I certainly don't go out more than a year though.

Of the middle school music teachers, Matt and Mike (both band) were the most structured in their planning and teaching. They dissected student repertoire and mathematically planned backward from the scheduled performance in order to appropriately pace students toward specific goals.

MATT: We're pretty big on clarity of expectations and helping students understand what we want them to know and be able to do at all times. Not just today, but two days from now, this week, this month, this trimester, this year . . . and we can take a kid who is coming into sixth grade and show them the homework for every week of all three years they are going to be there. Their concerts are the first week in May, so we'll project on the board each day the current tempos and final tempos for each piece. And basically what I do is get out a calculator and start making a schedule. We'll start rehearsing at half speed and just wait until all of the basic elements are in place—all the right notes, right rhythms, key signatures, articulations, dynamics—and it's only then that we start slowly speeding it up. We just do the math and figure out where we are and where we want to be, and we'll literally divide . . . we'll figure out how many beats per minute that may be—and maybe we're at 60 and we want to be at 120—then I'll just take the difference and divide that by the number of rehearsals and put right on the calendar how much faster it needs to be for each rehearsal. And then I project that on the board for the kids and they can see where we're supposed to be in that piece. Each day they can see how that's playing out in relation to the final tempos.

Mike's commentary focused on the larger, long-term goals he established for his students.

> MIKE: And I'm kind of weird that I have, typically, at least a three-year plan for each class. I begin with about a third of my students in the fifth grade (because I also teach at one feeder elementary school) so I use that to predict the future. I like to say, "I'd like to perform at this venue when these guys are in eighth grade" or "I'd like to do these tunes" or "I'd like to bring in these guest artists" or that kind of thing. That came up to my principal one time and she said that I was insane, because, "there's no way you can predict the future. You are trying to control things you can't control." And I said, "Well I like to prepare, so I'm reacting to things." But it's almost like a coaching position. I mean if you want to stay at that certain level, then you do have to kind of plan and prepare a set of reactions so you can sustain what you have.

Establishing Structure

Although some music educators operate in more structured ways than others, most will agree that even small acts of structure can be extremely beneficial for adolescent music students. Consider the simple step of supplying a daily agenda for students as they arrive to class. "When kids walk in the room, everyday the smart board says what we are doing today and what you need to do right now. When the bell rings [he claps], we're going!" (James, choir). Remember that for adolescents, knowledge is power. Any information that we can make available—such as a daily agenda—will provide adolescent music students with a sense of what is to come, a sense of partnership or inclusion in the music class, and a better understanding of the desired tone for music class or rehearsal.

When adolescent music students are faced with an unknown situation, such as the first day of class or a concert or festival experience, behavior can be unpredictable because students feel out of control of their surrounding circumstances. In such situations, structure *and* consistency can combat student unpredictability. Examples include phrasing instructions the same way each time, completing sight-reading exercises via the same order of steps, or always lining up on rises in the same way. "Consistency for me, or for those kids, leads to confidence. And I think if they are confident, it typically means that they are going to be more successful, as opposed to,

'I don't know what to expect, I'm nervous,' which leads to silly mistakes or inconsistent playing" (Mike, band).

To counteract unpredictability and encourage the idea of structure and consistency, one method is to practice chaos—helping students learn how to make themselves comfortable in less-than-ideal settings. In my own middle school classroom, I would take my choral students to atypical locations in the school where we rarely gathered as a choir, such as the echoey cafeteria, the compact area under the second-floor stairway, between the double doors in the school entranceways, or even outside the building on the front walkway. Students would stand around clumped in random groups until given a certain cue. From there, they would organize themselves in concert order and walk back to the choir room and onto the risers, as if beginning a performance. These simple exercises eliminated several future issues, as students were already used to settling down and organizing themselves in a strange place. Mike (band) prepared his students similarly:

> MIKE: You're not always performing in your band room; you're not always performing on your stage at school or your gym. You are at different festivals or have to warmup on the bus—we've had to warmup outside, we've had to warmup in stairwells ... that kind of thing. But regardless of *location*, everything else is consistent because we're doing the exact same thing and I'm talking the exact same way. So it's a little more soothing and calming for the students.

James (choir) followed a similar "practice chaos" protocol when it came time to have a substitute music teacher (he is Mr. Cumings in the following interview excerpt).

> JAMES: When I know I'm going to be gone and have a substitute teacher, we spend a class period (or at least half a class period) preparing for what it's going to be like when that substitute is here. I have student leaders who are in charge of warmups. I have student leaders who are in charge of taking attendance and a couple of different students who are in charge of sight-reading. And we practice what it's like to have our peers teach us, what it's like to have our peers give us correction, what it's like for us to support our peers when they don't lead as well or as quickly as when Mr. Cumings is here.

This entire notion of practicing chaos always reminds me of a scene from the 1986 sports movie *Hoosiers*. The story follows a small-town Indiana high school basketball team during the 1951–1952 academic year; this was a time when all high schools in Indiana, regardless of size, competed in one state championship tournament. The movie was inspired by the real-life 1954 high school basketball team from Milan, Indiana, the smallest school in state history to win Indiana's one-class basketball tournament (Johnson, 2013). The scene that I am referencing is when the small-town team arrives to the venue in Indianapolis for the championship game. They walk into the gym, which is absolutely enormous and expansive, especially in comparison to their home gym in Hickory, Indiana. Not a word is spoken as the players take in the magnitude of the space and the situation; it is clearly overwhelming to them. Coach Norman Dale (brilliantly played by Gene Hackman) pulls out a tape measure and asks one of his players to measure the distance from the backboard to the free-throw line, as well as the distance from the basketball rim to the court floor. He then says, "I think that you'll find it's the exact same measurements as our gym back in Hickory" (Daly & Anspaugh, 1986). The moral of the story for us as music educators is that our adolescent music students will be considerably more successful in different settings if there is something familiar for them to count on (structure) and from which to draw some comfort and confidence—regardless of the true significance of a musical event or performance space.

Returning to the idea of structure and flexibility in the music classroom: it's best to remember that we all "plot" differently on the x- and y-axes and there is no single right way of approaching our music classroom and students. Our first consideration should be the specific needs of our adolescent student populations within unique music teaching settings to determine the most beneficial approaches for everyone involved. From there, we can then meld those details with our individual philosophies of teaching adolescent music students, allowing us to more thoughtfully approach long-term preparations and short-term planning.

CLASSROOM MANAGEMENT AND DISCIPLINE

The terms "classroom management" and "discipline" are often used interchangeably, but they do have separate connotations. Classroom management is about being proactive and establishing structure (procedures, rules, consequences) at the beginning of the school year to maintain order throughout the year. Discipline is reactive as you respond to behaviors of your music students (as a result, students face consequences for their actions). Gary Rubinstein is a math teacher who addressed these two terms at the beginning of his book *Beyond Survival: How to Thrive in Middle and High School for Beginning and Improving Teachers*. "Classroom management is what a teacher does to *prevent* his students from misbehaving. Discipline is what a teacher must do when his students are misbehaving; discipline occurs after a student misbehaves" (Rubinstein 2011, 10, emphasis in original). My music education colleague at the University of Illinois, Jeananne Nichols, prefers the concept of "restoration" versus discipline. Rather than responding to adolescent student behavior with a perspective of punishment, perhaps the music student needs to be approached more with an attitude toward restoration and reinforcement of desired behavior. It is a nice idea.

Matters of classroom management and discipline must be considered on a case-by-case basis, for adolescents are unique and there is no one solution for navigating all student behavior issues. The uniqueness of every music teaching setting and situation means that classroom management and discipline cannot really be taught; however, the consideration of various approaches and views could be helpful for current and future music teachers of adolescents when designing individual classroom strategies. Humor will be discussed as a classroom management technique in chapter 6.

Classroom Management

The music teachers who contributed to this book spoke almost exclusively of classroom management and rarely even mentioned discipline and consequences. "Because if you have classroom management at the forefront, everything else falls into place. If you don't have classroom management, it doesn't matter what you are teaching—you can't teach" (Jason, band). Seth (choir) shared similar thoughts:

> SETH: When I have a class with 70 or 80 kids at a time, my word is law. And it has to be, otherwise we'd have complete chaos and nothing would get done. No education would happen so classroom management is strong. And that's the basis of all success with these performance groups—or any group. If you don't have classroom management, education isn't going to happen.

A cool twist to the conversation came when David (choir and guitar) shared valuable thoughts about the idea of classroom management as an important piece of *our* work as music educators—the importance of managing *ourselves* in the heat of the moments of teaching.

> DAVID: For a while, I actually put a picture of a swan on my music stand, swimming, because that was the image I wanted students to see. A very calm swan above the water and you could not see the legs moving like crazy underneath the water, which is what I don't want people to see. I don't want them to see my frustration; I don't want them to see a lot of things that are under the surface. So a lot of managing classes for me is managing myself and that's something I've learned over the years, and also from reading different things. I feel like that's important. If I cannot manage myself, then it's going to be very difficult for me to manage groups of people.

The Influence of Physical Space

Classroom management really begins even before students set foot in your space—it begins with considerations of the layout of your classroom. In *The Organized Teacher's Guide to Classroom Management*, authors Steve Springer and Kimberly Persiana stress the importance of the actual physical layout and organization of a classroom as an important component of classroom management. Consider the following questions with regard to how your classroom and space is currently used or how you envision using your future classroom space; below, I also provide my own music classroom adaptations of some of Springer and Persiana's questions in brackets:

- What do you do with it?
  - [Music classroom consideration: What various-sized groups will utilize your music classroom space?]
- How do you set it up?
- Where do the desks go?
  - [Music classroom consideration: Where do the chairs, risers, music stands, piano, instruments go?]
- Should you have a desk for the aide or volunteers?
  - [Music classroom consideration: Should you have a desk for the music student teacher?]
- Where do your supplies go?
- Do you need a rug area?
  - [Music classroom consideration: Do you need a rug area, as well as an open space of some sort? Do you need a riser area?]

- Do you need a teacher's desk?
- Will you organize learning centers?
  - [Music classroom consideration: Will you organize composition or music technology stations or small-ensemble spaces?]

  (Springer and Persiana 2011, 40)
- How does my classroom meet needs for:
  - Individual student work?
  - Students working in pairs?
  - Small groups?
  - Multiple types of instruction?
  - Multiple activities occurring at the same time?
  - Assessment?
  - Monitoring students?
  - Emergency situations?
  - Special needs of students? (Springer and Persiana 2011, 42)

Attention to these sorts of details can make a very big difference in the dynamic of your music classes; this is "structure" in a very tangible form. For a real-world example, let us consider three of my middle school teaching settings and then reexamine Springer and Persiana's questions with these settings in mind.

Schools A and B: During my first year as a music teacher, I taught at two junior high schools in the same school district; the schools were five miles apart from each other. My schedule was challenging: first hour at school A, second hour at school B, third hour at school A, fourth hour at school B—you get the picture. No planning period, no lunch period. Looking back, I recognize how problematic this situation was, but that is a discussion for another day. All that aside, I had to be completely proactive about classroom setup and procedures because there literally was no time to prepare anything when I arrived at each building for each class; thus I benefited greatly from all classroom management procedures I put into place at the start of the school year.

At school A, I shared a regular classroom with three other teachers who taught science, math, and Spanish. The room was located on the front side of the school and had many windows along the outside wall, as well as windows along the wall that faced the entrance hallway of the school; so two of the four walls of the classroom were windows and we had a clear view of anyone coming into or leaving the school. Each day when I arrived for my various classes, the desks were in different configurations depending on who was using the classroom before me. All music and books remained locked in the adjoining office to prevent theft or damage. Even though the piano had a lock on it, students in other classes broke the wood around the lock to pry open the keyboard cover and either play the piano or write on the keys. At school B I had a typical choir room that was attached to the school auditorium. It was a nice space, even though there were no windows (and, as a result, it got quite hot in there during warm months because the school did not have air conditioning); but the space was all mine. I kept music in unlocked file cabinets in my classroom and other materials locked in my adjoining office. We had a nice piano and access to the auditorium whenever we wished. The choir room was far away from other classrooms, so it was a quiet setting in which to work. I had no computer or phone at either school.

School C: The choir classroom where I taught for the majority of my public school years was *technically* a room, but in reality it was the cafetorium stage with a "soundproof" (note the quotation marks there) wall between cafeteria happenings and choir classes. The room was very long and narrow with less than great air circulation, especially on warm days. When choral risers were in use, there was the sense of much more room in that space than when the chairs were lined in rows (typically I had fifty to sixty Wenger chairs set up at a time to accommodate bigger classes). My office was located across the hall (a little former storage room within the cafeteria) where all music was stored, as was my desk, computer, and phone.

At school C, as the choir room was part of the cafeteria, morning preparations by the kitchen staff for the menu of the day sometimes influenced our classroom flow. For example, taco-prep mornings could be challenging as our room would reek of onions and taco seasoning; however, chocolate-chip-cookie Fridays were excruciatingly painful. Who can concentrate when all you can smell are warm, freshly baked chocolate chip cookies? During the three lunch periods, the noise from the cafeteria was almost overpowering through the "soundproof" wall.

Let's go back to the questions posed by Springer and Persiana about classroom setup. My response to each of these questions would differ depending on which of the three classrooms and school settings I was considering—even the two different settings within the same teaching position would elicit different answers. I agree with these authors that contemplation of classroom details is an important aspect of classroom management, because they not only help us to determine the most efficient way to set up our music classrooms but also lead us to consider additional organizational structures that need to be in place before students arrive. For example, if the room setup is not appropriate for your music class (as was a daily occurrence for me within the school A scenario above), what procedures must be in place for adolescent music students to understand their roles in preparing for class each day? What specific materials do they need to bring to class? When they arrive, how do they help—do they arrange desks or hand out folders? What attendance system is in place and what role do students play in those procedures? What happens at the end of class—do students return desks to their original formation prior to leaving the music classroom? Do chairs need to be stacked in the corner of the room or straightened in rows? How will classroom procedures differ if materials are stored out in the open versus if they are locked within cabinets and/or offices? If technology is used in your music class on a particular day—say, a classroom set of iPads—what classroom management procedures must be in place to preserve the integrity of the equipment and ensure a successful lesson? What potential problems are you warding off through consideration of all of these finer points?

As described in my classroom recollections above, every teaching venue has important sensory details that need to be taken into account just as much as the physical layout of the music classroom. Certain sensory details can distract adolescent students enough to immediately derail a music class or rehearsal and can include (but are not limited to):

- Room temperature and humidity: Is the room too hot or too cold? Also, regarding humidity, is it hot and sticky or dry? Humidity has implications for instruments and voices, as well as attention spans and fidgetiness.
- Scents: The emergence of adolescent body odor can be distracting; cafeteria/food smells; students wearing too much scented body spray that may be offensive or trigger allergies of scent-sensitive students and teachers.
- Noise: Additional noises or ambient sounds from outside of the music classroom; announcements over the school's speaker system; interruptions to music class, such as calling a student to the office; safety drills; squeaky risers. Also, how do acoustics of the music room impact rehearsals or classes? Are acoustics so dead or so live that having the concert performance in a different space will throw students off? Is your room so small or so live that students feel oppressed by the sound, leading to problematic behavior responses? Is the room so dead that you and your students push their voices to be heard, leading to problematic behavior responses from fatigue? Also, are room environments such that the students' and your hearing and/or voices could be compromised over time?
- Visual distractions: Is there a window through which kids will get distracted by all kinds of weather or people walking by? Is there a wall of mirrors in your room? Is there anything on the walls to distract or focus student attention? What is the lighting situation for the classroom?
- Proximity to others: How will students fit in your classroom space for their various activities, including procedures (getting instruments

out, moving to one's seat), musical-related actions (physical stretches and/or warmups at the beginning of class, rehearsals, changing seating positions for different pieces of music), and safety evacuations? Can everyone see the teacher? In what ways are sectionals or small group activities possible in this space?

Many environmental factors will influence the concentration and achievement levels of adolescent music students, which in turn affect motivation, participation, and behavior. In order to keep potential problems at bay, it is sensible to consider all kinds of music classroom details—right down to the senses—and develop classroom management strategies to proactively address and navigate such items before even beginning with your adolescent music students.

Student Engagement

I have this whole idea about classroom management that if a student's engaged then they don't have enough brainpower to also be a problem. (Marsha, band)

There was general consensus among the music teachers that student engagement is one of the best forms of classroom management, as desirable student behavior is almost always an outcome. For James (choir), "Students no longer engaged in the task at hand get creative in all the wrong directions." When Matthew's (band) students misbehave, he finds that it is typically for one of two reasons that are rooted in lack of engagement in the music classroom:

MATTHEW: One, boredom, which means their needs aren't being met, they could do more, and they are off-task because they've accomplished what you want them to; or two, frustration, which means I don't understand, I'm missing something, I'm listening, I'm really trying, but I'm unsuccessful and there's only going to be a limit for how much I'm really going to try for you. But if this continues, then I'm going to disengage. I'm going to get somebody else off-task because this is no longer meaningful or purposeful to me.

Pacing was noted as an important element of student engagement, as was the balance of "teacher talking" versus "students doing." As music educators, our goal is for students to experience music on a variety of levels, not to listen to us pontificate about various topics. With shorter attention spans—complicated by students' instant-gratification world of texting, YouTube, Twitter, Instagram, and so forth—adolescents will begin to tune us out after about ten minutes. As discussed in chapter 1, and relevant here as well, it is in our best interest (and that of our students) to limit lectures or instructions to around five minutes, followed by ten to fifteen minutes of students *doing* (such as listening, singing, playing, composing, improvising); repeat.

One of the most important components of student engagement in the adolescent music class is a connection between the topic or task at hand to the students' larger well-being. If adolescents do not deem something meaningful or purposeful to their greater selves—if they do not see the point as to why they should know or understand something—then they will disengage and, most often, misbehave.

Interacting with Adolescent Music Students

Learning students' names and greeting them at the music classroom door is an excellent, proactive approach toward classroom management. Taking time to talk to students one on one—even just in passing—is an important part of forming relationships and trust. It is a means of reaffirming to individual music students that they matter, which is key during adolescent years because everyone wants to feel that they belong or fit in *somewhere*. In addition, supplementary contact with music students results in richer relationships with them. Not only do you learn more about them over time, it provides students an opportunity to get to know *you* in a slightly different way, which can positively impact students' perceptions of you as a person as well as a music teacher.

As discussed earlier in this book, adolescent misbehavior can stem from many causes, both outside and inside the music classroom. Maintaining an awareness of potential causes or influential factors is proactive classroom management. Factors *outside* of the classroom that could influence student behavior within the classroom include lack of sleep, shuffling between two homes because of divorced parents, an inadequate breakfast and/or poor nutrition, an argument with a sibling or parent before coming to school, lack of a quiet place to study, living in an abusive home situation, problems with classmates or other school peers, and/or too much time spent in extracurricular activities and not enough time dedicated to schoolwork. Factors *within* the classroom that could potentially influence student behavior include not enough exposure to/background experience with the curriculum, insufficient English-language ability, a low level of subject-specific mastery, lack of materials and books, lack of support for new or difficult concepts, diagnosed special needs, benchmarks that are not being considered when instruction is planned and delivered, and/or misunderstanding or disregard for the student's learning styles and interests by the teacher (Springer and Persiana, 2011).

Therefore, the more that we interact with our adolescent music students, the more we can form a baseline understanding about individual students' behaviors when discipline issues arise. If an incident seems out of character for a particular student in our music classes, chances are that something is happening elsewhere in their lives (outside the music classroom and/or inside the music classroom) that is influencing them. From these prior interactions, we are better prepared to make general determinations about the situation and act (or react) more appropriately to the circumstances and help our student.

Discipline

More often, newer music teachers uphold a larger number of rules and consequences for their students than do more seasoned teachers—my own early-career list of classroom rules was meticulously long and detailed. With time and experience such lists most often boil down to the nitty-gritty. My own exhaustive list of rules eventually became two broad expectations: (1) Respect (applied to all people, places, and property); and (2) follow the Golden Rule: treat others as you would like to be treated. Violations of these two rules were dealt with on a case-by-case basis, but policies were upheld consistently across the board; more on this in a moment. James (choir) upheld a similar approach to mine in his own choir classroom:

> JAMES: One is that you show respect to your friends, yourself, your teacher or adults, and the music that we do. We talk about what that means with your peers, showing each other respect and love, what that mean for adults, me, substitutes, anyone that comes in. What does it mean to show respect to your music? And they're usually like, "Well, don't tear it up and don't fold it." They're thinking tangibly. So then we talk about, "What does it mean when we're performing a song that you may not like but the neighbor next to you loves? What does it mean to show respect for your art?" and that sort. So there's that. And then the second rule is to try and do

your best at all times, in everything that we do. Do your best and work at it. And everyday we work with those two rules.

Expectations such as "respect" and "follow the Golden Rule" place the responsibility of student behavior in the students' hands and become much less about our maintaining a list of rules for students to follow and more about empowering students to control how they would like to be treated in the music classroom. With my middle school choir students, management strategies were aimed toward building students' repertoire of appropriate behaviors versus punishing students who were behaving badly. Although consequences existed for violations of respect, there became less of a need for punishment as students took ownership and responsibility for themselves and their actions.

Part of our responsibility as music teachers is to show adolescent students that we care, even if that means upholding classroom rules and policies "against" them to teach and protect them. Although the following excerpt from *Not Much Just Chillin'* was written for parents, it absolutely applies to our work as music teachers (as you can see from my addition of the words "music teachers" each time the author mentions "parents").

> It may not look like it, but a middle schooler wants to be told no. If she hears it from an early age, she'll be used to it when the stakes are raised. She wants rules—which sometimes get her out of situations she isn't comfortable being in anyway. Okay, maybe she doesn't *always* want rules, maybe she despises the rules. But psychologists insist that parents [music teachers] should persist anyway, because, in ten, twenty, thirty years, secure, successful adults say they appreciate their childhood rules, in retrospect. Even if the kids whose parents [music teachers] set strong, reasonable ethical and moral limits may experiment, they're likelier to drift back eventually within the standards their parents [music teachers] tried to enforce. They turn out better, simply put. Even if she resists them outwardly, a child with strong connections to adult authority figures becomes stronger herself, more in control. Kids whose parents [music teachers] have distanced themselves are far more susceptible to peer pressure and more likely to misbehave in school. (Perlstein 2003, 100)

Generally speaking, you will hear one of two things from adolescents: (1) "I hate my parents/teachers for [fill in the reason: e.g., giving me a curfew]. They never let me do anything"; or (2) "I hate my parents/teachers. They don't care enough about me to [fill in the blank; e.g., give me a curfew]." It is more advantageous to have a student mad because we are consistent with rules and consequences than because we are not consistent. "I don't make empty threats, I make promises. And I follow through with what I say I'm going to do. And they know that" (Michelle, choir).

Adolescent music students benefit most from teachers who uphold students to high personal and professional standards. James (choir) believes in being "insistent, persistent, and consistent" in his dealings with *all* of his middle school students—even the best ones.

> JAMES: And it's hard, especially when your good kid screws up and you've got to nail them just like you would the kid that drives you nuts. They know where the line is and they know if they cross it. And if they cross it, they already know the consequence. Kids function really well in an environment like that. I remember hearing a study about a schoolyard and they took out all the fences and all the kids played really close in this one little area. And then they put a huge fence around the entire schoolyard and the kids played everywhere in the yard because they knew where the fence was and they felt safe inside that. So I think that a great deal of structure can allow kids the freedom to work within that structure and know the boundaries.

I had a rule in my middle school choir classes that if you pulled a chair out from underneath another student (as described earlier, my choir room had rows of Wenger chairs), you automatically went to In-School Suspension (ISS) and were not allowed to attend the next extracurricular school function, such as a dance or a sporting event. Steven was a tall, blond, soft-spoken, wonderful student who got great grades, was adored by all of his peer groups and teachers, and just a genuinely nice person. Steven *never* got into trouble. One day, he was playfully screwing around with a couple of the other boys in the choir room as adolescents do, and he pulled a chair out from underneath a classmate who fell hard on the floor and hit his head on the chair that Steven was holding. It was as if a record player arm was suddenly scratched off of a record and the entire room *froze*, looking at me, waiting for me to react. Steven's eyes *pleaded* with me, "Please don't send me to ISS! I didn't mean it!" But I *had to*. Every student was waiting to see what I would do and it broke my heart. "Steven I *have* to send you to ISS now. The rule is that we never pull chairs out from under each other because people get hurt and that's what's happened." It was really hard, but I know that my students respected my upholding discipline policies in the same way for *all* students.

Although a number of disciplinary techniques can be employed in our adolescent music classes, it is imperative that *music* never be used as a punishment for student behavior. As music educators, we want our students to learn from all of their experiences, including those involving discipline; associating music or performance with a punishment defeats all of our good work. "I will never punish my kids with singing. Ever. I will *never* say something like, 'Well, Tommy you didn't sing in choir today so tomorrow you have to come in and sing all the repertoire in front of everyone'" (Michelle, choir).

The music teachers overwhelmingly disqualified yelling as an effective disciplinary tool, as adolescents took it mostly as a lack of respect toward them and then lost respect for the yelling teacher. Rather, according to Springer and Persiana (2011), more effective techniques for managing adolescent student behavior—and redirecting behavior away from situations that require overt discipline—can include nonverbal cues, moving the activity along [pacing], group focus, behavior redirection, needed instruction [preteach or reteach], a brief halt, offering a choice, withholding a privilege, isolation or removal of students, and/or referral to the school office [as a last resort] (Springer and Persiana 2011, 98). Ignoring the behavior altogether is another option in certain circumstances. Several of the interviewed teachers also stand by the use of a good "teacher look." Kate (general music) specifically calls hers the "Hairy Eyeball."

For me, I have always been a big fan of proximity when working with adolescent music students because I can navigate and redirect so many classroom issues without having to stop what I am teaching in the process. I found similar sentiments in the book *The Journey from Music Student to Teacher* by music education professors Michael Raiber and David Teachout:

One of the most effective tools available for engaging students, and often one of the most underused, is the act of varying one's proximity to the students. Because most teachers remain in the front of the room for the duration of the class period, those teachers who choose to move throughout the room will automatically raise students' attention by piquing their curiosity. When movement becomes deliberate, purposeful, and strategic, student engagement improves significantly. For example, approaching an off-task student and simply delivering your content while standing beside the student's chair will most likely result in the student changing behaviors. Further, this subtle type of communication gives the student the opportunity to self-regulate his behavior without being called out by the teacher, and it allows the teacher to continue teaching without interrupting the flow of the lesson (Raiber and Teachout 2014, 109).

Interacting with Parents of Adolescents

The middle school music teachers discussed the involvement of students' parents as a successful tool or strategy toward managing student behavior. Below, Michelle (choir) and Kate (general music) share their insight on calling parents.

> MICHELLE: Calling parents is the best thing in the world. And when I call them I will say things like, "I really appreciate all the time that you spend with your kid. What would you recommend I do to help the situation? What do you use at home?" The parents often feel like it's a personal attack on them when you call them on their kid. Because of that, I do try to call parents and tell them when their kids are doing great. Every kid is good. *Every kid is good.* You've just got to figure out where it is and what it is. They're not bad kids. They're kids!

> KATE: I've found that I have much more power if I deal with an issue within my own classroom. And I've been known to call a parent, like *(snap!)* right there during class. I don't have a phone in my classroom; I use my cell phone and call in the middle of class. And when I do that, the rest of the students will just sit and wait. I hate wasting time with them, but sometimes that phone call is all a student needs so they know that they are not going to talk to that other kid like that; they are not going to be a bully. Most of the time they get the consequence at home and don't cross me again. A lot of that is in sixth grade. I don't have to make a lot of parent phone calls in seventh or eighth grade because I made them in sixth.

> BRIDGET: Do you ever have the parent talk to the child?

> KATE: We go into the hallway and usually I say *(motioning as if handing over the phone to the student)*, "You are going to tell them what just happened. I'm going to dial your mom, here's the phone." Yeah, it works.

Contrary to Michelle and Kate's successful experiences with calling parents, Bethany (general music) found calling parents to rarely be helpful with her population of music students. In fact, her principal often advised her to not call specific parents because of potential ramifications of such a call for individual students at home or for the school as a whole.

BETHANY: Sometimes the principal will say to me, "Don't call that parent because it will be even more of a problem. That parent is on drugs (or whatever). We don't want them to come up here to the school when they're on drugs." So it can be crazy.

Adolescent music students have their own perspectives and expectations about teachers calling their parents as a disciplinary tactic. As discussed by middle schoolers Alma and Amelia in *Fires in the Middle School Bathroom,* calling home should be done in moderation and determined by situational circumstances.

ALMA: A thing a lot of teachers make a mistake on, at least in my perspective, is that they call the parents for really little things. In my math class, there was a minor problem that my teacher could have solved right there and then. She called my parents. That makes us feel like we can't trust the teacher, you know? 'Cause some things are really personal. Some things kids don't even want to share with their family. What if it's *about* their family? (Cushman and Rogers 2008, 156–57)

AMELIA: If teachers got to know the parents better, they would know how to deal with kids when they're acting up. Kids go, "Oh yeah, call my parents, I don't care." They get into trouble and they still do it again. But if you got to know their parents and made friends with them, then probably the kids wouldn't act up. (ibid., 2008, 157)

Alma and Amelia make good points in their comments here, first being that an overzealous calling of parents can be problematic for all involved parties. Secondly, just as we benefit from getting to know our students on a deeper level, we also benefit from getting to know our music students' parents and guardians. It is important to keep in mind during interactions with parents and family members that, as educators, we should never make assumptions about our students' parents or family situation based on behaviors of the adolescent (or of the adolescent, based on parent behavior). We should never assume that a naughty music student has a parent who does not care or does not work hard for the success of their child. Most parents work immensely hard to provide as much opportunity as possible for their children. By getting to know parents and working *with* parents, we gain a much clearer and honest picture of how to best work with individual adolescents, especially with regard to discipline in our music classrooms.

Communication with our music students' families need not *only* be about discipline problems. On the contrary, positive contact will strengthen relationships with parents, as well as students, as you will be perceived as a teacher who cares about the overall well-being of your music students.

> MARSHA (BAND): Interacting with parents is *so* important, and building a positive rapport with parents and recognizing students for good things (especially at the middle-school level) helps to build a trusting relationship. I feel like parents, in general, don't get enough of those good phone calls. Parents have good kids. I think most of them know that they have good kids, but they never really get that reassurance of, "Hey, you're doing the right thing." Also that communication with parents lets the kids know, "Hey, Ms. Miller is checking in with my dad every so often." So I make it a point once a month to pick out five or six kids who I thought were doing something really great and either call or send an email home. "Alright, it's the 20th. I get paid today and now I need to do some positive phone calls, get some positive parental interactions going on!" *(laughs)*

In the grand scheme of things, a quick positive phone call or note home can often make more positive strides towards desired student behavior than several negative calls home. Here are a few added tips for interacting with students' families from *The Organized Teacher's Guide to Classroom Management* (Springer and Persiana 2011, 101):

- Contact parents regularly (within reason) about a student's behavior problem before it is necessary to conference with them
- Offer several choices for a meeting time—before school, after school, or even by phone
- Have documentation about the adolescent's pattern of behavior available to refer to during the conference. This documentation can be in the form of anecdotal notes, weekly progress reports, referral notices, a log of phone calls home, or interventions by another teacher or an administrator.
- Ways to communicate with parents:
  ◦ Weekly, bimonthly, or monthly newsletter home
  ◦ Teacher's website
  ◦ Email (use your school email address and not your personal one)
  ◦ Phone calls home (to maintain professionalism and to avoid revealing your personal phone number via caller ID, use the school phone)
  ◦ Inviting parents to visit the music classroom

- Set boundaries, with designated times and days
- Parents must always sign in at the office
- Check school and/or district policies
  - Requesting parent volunteers
    - Volunteers need school and/or district clearance
    - Check school and/or district policies
    - Volunteers usually need medical clearance (for example, negative TB tests)
    - It may be better for parents not to volunteer in their own child's classroom, but in another classroom at the same grade level
  - Weekly progress report

Preserving Student Dignity

They will do as you ask if they trust you and know that you are there for them. An environment of trust goes a long way in the learning process. (Marsha, band)

Our actions and words speak loudly to music students and, along with that, there are appropriate ways, times, and places for disciplining our young adolescents. In *SongWorks 1: Singing in the Education of Children*, music educators Peggy D. Bennett and Douglas R. Bartholomew wrote about the importance of "a moment of grace" when addressing instances of student misbehavior:

A moment of grace is the interval of time we take to reframe someone's behavior so that we can react with curiosity, compassion, or openness rather than judgment, annoyance, or defensiveness. Giving someone the "benefit of the doubt" allows us to delay our reaction to the comment or action with the intent of looking beyond our immediate response. This form of second-guessing can serve several constructive purposes: It can help us avoid responding in ways that we may later regret, it can help us look further into sometimes innocent reasons for the behavior, and it can help us develop a habit of openness to varying levels and dimensions of understanding others. (Bennett and Bartholomew 1997, 210)

Along these same lines, it is also imperative to remember who is being disciplined and not take frustration out on other music students who had nothing to do with the situation.

Something else to consider is the idea of allowing adolescents to save face in front of their peers when they are being disciplined. This is important in the music classroom because it upholds the expectation of "respect for others"—so even though the naughty kid will be disciplined, he or she will still be treated with respect. From *Discipline with Dignity*:

> It is important to avoid power struggles that emerge when a student needs to save face with peers. Public displays of consequence implementation embarrass the student and often make it difficult for the student to hear the message. Although avoiding a public conflict is sometimes impossible, privacy in implementing consequences is a helpful way for all to save face. Remember, your goal is to keep teaching, and you need to minimize words or gestures to get the message across without worsening the situation. Shielding the rule breaker from public embarrassment will give all of the other students in class the message that their right to privacy will be maintained, that their integrity will be preserved, and that they are expected to behave in class. (Curwin, Mendler, and Mendler 2008, 113–14)

Kate (general music) and David (choir and guitar) shared similar thoughts about maintaining privacy for their music students during dealings of discipline.

> KATE: Usually I take them out into the hallway. I don't like to make a spectacle of it, usually. Because I have to be quite specific about what happened and in order to do that, I don't feel like I can do that in front of the other children. Everyone doesn't exactly need to know what went down.
>
> DAVID: I try to talk with them and not at them. I want them to know that, "I'm a little bit disappointed about this specific thing, not about you as a person" or "when you demonstrate this behavior it really does disappoint me, I have to be honest with you," that type of thing. And I find that that brings good results with the students that I'm working with as opposed to calling them out in front of other people. I try to bypass the social structure of the choir, which can be very difficult, because if you embarrass someone, you'll not only have that person mad at you, but you'll also have forty-five other people mad at you.

Jay's (choir and composition) philosophy of classroom discipline is that teachers must not punish without certainty, which is admirable and goes a long way with adolescent music students. In his words:

> JAY: I try to follow a simple rule: do not punish without certainty. In a classroom, one of four scenarios can play out: (1) The student

does something good and the teacher praises the student. (2) The student does something bad and the teacher scolds the student. (3) The student does something bad and the teacher mistakenly praises the student. (4) The student does something good and the teacher mistakenly scolds the student. The first two scenarios are supposed to happen. The last two should not happen, but should one of them happen, it must be the third scenario. If a teacher mistakenly praises bad behavior, the student will forgive them; but if a teacher mistakenly scolds a student, the student will never forgive or forget. The bottom line is this: students crave routine, structure, and fairness. They may fight it individually when they get called upon, but they welcome it and are even proud of being a part of such a class.

Bullying in the Music Classroom

Disciplinary tactics *should* differ when dealing with instances of student bullying. Navigating the issue of bullying with young adolescents can be tricky, as it tends to take form as a group mentality against one or two individual students. Linda Perlstein writes about this in *Not Much Just Chillin'*:

> Bullying awareness programs are predicated on a false, almost quaint notion: that the "them," the bullies standing ready to take your lunch money and your dignity, are a minority, vultures who can be ignored or disciplined into quiescence. In fact, though, the primary form of bullying in middle school is not shoving or threatening but excluding from the group. The bullied are the small number (usually the aggressive, or the withdrawn) and the bullies nearly everyone else, who—empowered by groupthink, tinged by guilt over abandoning their Do Unto Others values but not so much so as to trump the overwhelming desire to belong—poke and prod these chosen victims more often than not in subtle, gossipy, tiny ways; ways impossible to legislate away or even, often, to notice. (Perlstein 2003, 109)

Earlier we reflected upon the reality that adolescents are emotional and can lash out in situation X as a response to something that happened during situation Y. Danah Boyd associates this adolescent characteristic with bullying in her book *It's Complicated: The Social Lives of Networked Teens.* She does not make excuses for bullying—far from it—but in the chapter "Bullying: Is Social Media Amplifying Meanness and Cruelty?" she acknowledges that bullying is a complicated and multifaceted issue with modern, networked teenagers, and oftentimes it is actually a reaction to something else in the bully's life. Her entire conversation is quite thought-provoking but too complex to paraphrase here; however, the following short passage provides perspective to our current discussion on bullying in music classrooms:

> Bullies are not evil people who decide to torment for fun; those are sociopaths. Most bullies react aggressively because they're struggling with serious issues of their own. Many teens lash out when they are trying to negotiate serious identity or mental health issues. Other are reacting to abuse at home. It's easy to empathize with those who are on the receiving end of meanness and cruelty. It's much harder—and yet perhaps more important—to offer empathy to those who are doing the attacking. (Boyd 2014, 135)

Although it is unrealistic to think that we will be able to prevent all instances of such behaviors inside and outside of our music classrooms, the more that we know our students—including what constitutes "normal" behavior for individuals—the more we can be proactive about providing assistance to struggling students. Perhaps our efforts will steer a struggling student toward channeling their negative energy in more productive directions versus bullying a fellow music student.

As teachers of adolescent music students, it is important to know what the ramifications of bullying might look like in real time in our classrooms. Music educator Bruce Carter has identified behaviors commonly exhibited by students being harassed or bullied in his article "A Safe Education for All: Recognizing and Stemming Harassment in Music Classes and Ensembles," including:

- Shows signs of bullying
- Is increasingly withdrawn or wanting to be alone
- Experiences significant drop in grades
- Has unexplained injuries, bruises, or cuts
- Arrives to class with torn, damaged, or missing clothing and belongings
- Is uncomfortable with peers
- Has no or few friends
- Has a difficult time defending himself or herself
- May pretend that nothing is wrong because of feelings of humiliation
- May claim to be ill, and ask to be excused from class. (Carter 2011, 31)

Carter encourages awareness of antibullying policies and procedures at school, county, and state levels, as well as nationally. Currently, what is your awareness of your school's policy on harassment and/or its antibullying policy? What is your awareness of county and/or state policies on such matters? How do these policies align with those in your own music classroom? It is good to be cognizant of official strategies so that you are well informed and well prepared when the situation arises, as it is highly likely that you will come face to face with some sort of bullying incident, if you have not already. Just always remember that as music educators (and decent human beings) it is our legal and ethical responsibility to take action against any instances of harassment and bullying, no matter how small or how big.

Veteran high school art educator Stacey Gross has trained teachers about counterbullying techniques through her presentation "That's SO Gay: How to Address Homophobia in Schools." As part of her presentation, Stacey adapted the Gay, Lesbian and Straight Education Network's (www.glsen.org) strategies for addressing hallway harassment into a section, "Effectively Address Harassment in Four Easy Steps," which applies to any bullying situation:

Step 1. *Stop the Harassment*
    Interrupt the comment. Halt the harassment.
    Make sure everyone in the vicinity can hear you. You want everyone—all the youth and adults nearby—to know that *all* young people are safe in this place.
    Do *NOT* pull the bully aside for a confidential discussion—stopping the harassment should be as public as the harassment has been.

Step 2. *Identify the Harassment*
    "You just put someone down regarding _____ (sexual orientation, gender expression, etc.)." or "You just shoved someone."
    Put the spotlight on the bully's behavior.
    Do *NOT* say anything to imply that the person being harassed belongs to the group just named. Everyone needs to understand that what was said or done is unacceptable.

Step 3. *Publicly Broaden the Response*
    Identify the offense and its consequences: "Name calling is hurtful to everyone who hears it." "Physical attacks on anyone are totally unacceptable and can result in the attacker facing consequences."
    Make it clear that the entire school is solidly opposed to such behavior. "In this school, we do not harass other people. Period." "In this school, any physical attack is totally unacceptable. Any repetition will have serious consequences for you."

Step 4. *Request a Change in Future Behavior*

Personalize the response for the bully: "Taylor, please think about what you say. This language isn't what I would have expected from you." "Jamie, by name-calling, you are being a bully. I don't want to hear that anymore from you."

Quietly check in with the person who was harassed.

Quietly reassure the person who was harassed: "Please let me know if this happens again, and I will take further action. What happened was unacceptable and you are very important to this class/school/team."

Again, consistency is critically important because your adolescent students will be watching how you handle bullying. If you allow incidents to occur unaddressed, your lack of handling the situation makes a clear statement that certain undesirable behaviors are acceptable. Such action on the part of the music teacher can be detrimental to adolescent music students (especially those on the receiving end of bullying) and ruin the sense of safe place and trust in your classroom. Upholding standards and expectations of respect by constantly and consistently addressing the many small issues that arise results in better relationships with your students and more efficient music classrooms. In addition, such efforts on your part often prevent small issues from turning into bigger ones.

DIGEST

There is much to consider regarding the structure of one's music classroom. As you read through chapter 4, perhaps you felt validated or reaffirmed about the methods that you have chosen to use in your current classroom. Or perhaps you developed interest in trying something new. All of the topics in this chapter should be considered fluid and changeable, depending upon classroom setting, group of students, or desired goals. Ultimately, it is most important to remember that there is no *one way* to teach adolescent music students.

CHAPTER 5

The Humanity of Teaching Music

When I was in college, I worked part-time at a sporting goods store. There was a kid who would come by two or three times a week to visit with this baseball mitt that he wanted to buy. My manager and I would joke about him not only because he was so dedicated and persistent, but also because he had picked the best and most expensive mitt in the shop to get obsessed about.

This went on for months. The kid would come in and you could tell he was so relieved that the mitt was still there. He would put it on, pound his fist into the pocket a couple of times, and then very carefully put it back onto the shelf and leave. Finally, one day he came in with a shoebox and a smile about eight miles wide and announced that he wanted to buy the mitt. So the manager brought the mitt over to the cash register while the kid counted out a shoebox worth of nickels, quarters, and dimes. His stash came to exactly $19.98.

The mitt cost $79.98, not including tax. My manager looked at the price tag, and sure enough the 7 was a little smudged, enough that a desperately hopeful seven-year-old could imagine it to be a 1. Then he looked at me, smiled, and very carefully recounted. "Yep, exactly $19.98." Wrapping up the mitt, he gave it to the boy.

(Random Acts of Kindness, 1993, 106–7)

Merriam-Webster defines humanity as "the quality or state of being kind to other people or to animals."[1] Through our music classes we have an incredible opportunity to teach adolescents not only about music but also about being kind people. Music education professor Paul Woodford writes in his book *Democracy and Music Education* that music teachers are as responsible for educating students about their own values, choices, beliefs, and ideas as they are for educating them about music. "Unless children learn how to do this, they will not be able to understand the issues or exert intelligent control over their own musical lives, much less contribute to the improvement of the human condition" (Woodford 2005, 31). Mike (band) commented, "I think that character development is as important as musical development." It is hard to argue with that. I have witnessed the power that discussions and meaningful student experiences can have on adolescent insight about human decency—especially within the realm of a music class. It is extraordinary to witness.

The work of middle school choral teacher Deb Borton was a driving force behind the creation of this book.[2] This chapter in particular is inspired by her work with adolescents, helping them to develop incredible musicianship skills *as well as* to become caring and empathetic citizens. Deb's work affirms that you don't have to sacrifice one for the other—that you *can* influence both through the music classroom. When open to such an approach to teaching music, opportunities to be ambassadors for good can be found just about anywhere. It is my hope that from a discussion of Deb's work, as well as the work of other music teachers, you are inspired to explore such avenues with adolescent music students within your own music classrooms.

S.P.A.M.: SINGING PRODUCES AWESOME MIRACLES

"Singing Produces Awesome Miracles" is Deb's motto for her middle school choir program, affectionately known as S.P.A.M. In addition, her association of the acronym S.P.A.M. with the Hormel pork product SPAM© has been fully embraced by her students. Hundreds of SPAM© logo signs, magnets, and pictures decorate her choir room and office; all choir students purchase a SPAM© logo t-shirt and wear it to school on the day of a choral concert. Each year Deb writes a SPAM©-themed parody song for the Extravaganza concert that talks about how singing produces awesome miracles. Past pieces have included renditions of "My Favorite Things," "Fame," and "Mr. Spam-man." The following lyrics were sung to the melody of the song *Y.M.C.A.* by the Village People:

Young man, here is something to eat,
We said, young man, it is really a treat.
We said, young man, when you're ready to dine,
There's no need to go away hungry.

Young man, try some SPAM© if you dare.
We said, young man, it'll curl your hair
You can fry it, top it off with some cheese;
Take a bite; it's sure to please you.

Come on, and join us for S.-P.-A.-M.
Can you believe it? It's S.-P.-A.-M.
It is made out of pork; at least that's what they say,
Won't you give it a try today?

Come on and join us for S.-P.-A.-M.
You're gonna love to eat S.-P.-A.-M.
Try a SPAM© pizza pie or maybe SPAM© stir-fry;
We just eat it and don't ask why.

Young man, SPAM© is really good!
We'd like to eat it every day if we could.
If I could somehow say that with a straight face,
It could help my grade in choir.

Young man, whatever it's called,
Singing Produces Awesome Miracles.
So thanks for coming to our concert tonight,
'Cause we love performing for you!

Come on, and join us for S.-P.-A.-M.
Can you believe it? It's S.-P.-A.-M.
It is made out of pork; at least that's what they say,
Won't you give it a try today?

Come on and join us for S.-P.-A.-M.
You're gonna love to eat S.-P.-A.-M.
Try a SPAM© pizza pie or maybe SPAM© stir-fry;
We just eat it and don't ask why.
Come on and join us for S.P.A.M.!

Deb's motto was originally created as a hook to get her sixth grade choral exploratory students to reenroll in seventh grade choir:

DEB: For me, the idea of my sixth grade exploratory classes is to get them hooked on singing in this room. I want them to be part of my program and they want to see that middle school *singing* is different than elementary music. So many kids come out of elementary school believing that music sucks and that it's boring and thank God they're done with that. I want them to go, "Oh my gosh! Yeah! This is cool! I like what the teacher's doing and singing really is cool!" That's the S.P.A.M. thing. There's something about it that grabs a kid of that age.

Not surprisingly, S.P.A.M. has been incredibly catchy. However, it also has become symbolic for doing something nice for other people, as the acronym was partially created in tribute to Deb's late father who worked at the Hormel factory in Austin, Minnesota. His job was to clean up butchered animal parts that fell on the floor of the factory every day. Although he absolutely hated his job, he continued to work there so that Deb could go to college. Her students shared with me: "That meant a lot to her so she made it into the acronym for our choir. And ever since then we've been touring around doing nice things for people, letting people know that Singing Produces Awesome Miracles." I interviewed a group of young women in Deb's eighth grade choir who spoke fondly of S.P.A.M. and shared stories of the miracles that they associated with choir and singing.

BRIDGET: Talk to me about S.P.A.M.

EVELYN: It rocks.

SOPHIA: Best thing *ever*. *(All the girls talk at once in excited voices.)* I thought it was so cool . . . I love how she came up with that! I love how she's actually from Minnesota and made the acronym and everything.

EVELYN: I think it kind of does represent what it says. Like, produces awesome miracles . . . it really *does*.

AVA: Yeah, I think singing does help. Like last year, my voice was *not* strong and I think that the miracle for me was that it actually got stronger and I got *so* over my nerves.

EVELYN: I think that was the miracle for me, too. I just have so much more confidence. *(All the girls immediately start telling Evelyn how much she has improved and complimenting her singing and newly gained confidence in singing.)*

JUNIPER: But I think one of the miracles is actually Mrs. Borton because she does so much for us.

LILLIAN: I think singing also produces miracles because it makes you *feel* so good when you sing. I'll have a really bad day and I think it's awesome because singing is just like . . . it's like a *feel-good* factor.

This intense manifestation of a choir motto works for Deb in her specific teaching setting. And although not all adolescent music students will embrace the specific motto, "Singing Produces Awesome Miracles," the idea of maintaining a core idea or value across a music program is important to adolescents who tend to be naturally drawn to the idea of belonging to or having membership in something bigger than them. "Young adolescents are striving to be part of the group because the alternative is feeling unwelcome, isolated, and lonely" (McMahan 2009, 185). John Cottere wrote in *Social Networks in Youth and Adolescence*:

> Membership refers to the sense of shared belonging and personal relatedness to the school. Through membership each person is associated with others, identifies with the larger group, and gains emotional security from that knowledge. When people value their membership and that of others, the very act of valuing reinforces their status and place as part of the school, thus integrating them into the institution. (Cottere 2007, 204)

Michelle (choir) calls this "getting the kids to drink the Kool-Aid." And once adolescents are on board with an idea, they are fiercely loyal to it.

RANDOM ACTS OF KINDNESS

A core component of S.P.A.M. is the practice of random acts of kindness, defined by Deb as "things that are done for no reward." In her classroom, students hear about random acts of kindness almost daily, including when she reads stories from the book *Random Acts of Kindness*.[3] After reading, Deb typically holds a brief conversation with her students as a way to solidify ideas about being kind to others. One of Deb's favorite stories is that of the Magic Dragon:

> Several years ago, when I was living in Chicago, I read in the newspaper about a little boy who had leukemia. Every time he was feeling discouraged or particularly sick, a package would arrive for him containing some little toy or book to cheer him up, with a note saying the present was from the Magic Dragon. No one knew who it was. Eventually the boy died, and his parents thought the Magic Dragon finally would come forth and reveal him or herself. But that never happened. After hearing the story, I resolved to become a Magic Dragon whenever I could, and I have had many occasions. (*Random Acts of Kindness* 2013, 158)

Deb often references the Magic Dragon story, especially when she is aware that someone at her school is hurting or grieving. For example, the mother of a fellow teacher passed away and, after reading the story to her sixth grade students, Deb discussed what it means to be a Magic Dragon.

> DEB: This story hits me where I live. Boys and girls, there is a teacher walking around today who has lost their mother. It doesn't matter who it is. Their heart is broken today. There is probably a student here at our middle school whose parent is sick or whose parents are divorcing and their heart is broken. It is YOUR choice to put your dragon on.

I penned the following vignette after Deb took her students Valentine caroling at a senior center on Valentine's Day. It was a very special day for all involved and provided her students with a tangible experience of how they can "produce awesome miracles" through acts of kindness with music:

> "Happy Valentine's Day!" The senior citizens smile and welcome Deb and the Varsity Choir members to the Senior Center. It is Thursday, February 14 and the students are dressed up in shades of pink and red. Many of the senior citizens also wear Valentine colors and several ladies show off heart-shaped jewelry. The students carry pink papers on which words of love songs are typed in 14-point font. The middle school students are not here to perform, but to sing with the people at the Senior Center.
>
> The second year of Valentine's Day caroling has drawn a large crowd to the Center and everyone is excited. In fact, although the Senior Center did not serve lunch yesterday, the Center ladies met and baked dozens of heart-shaped sugar cookies in preparation for today's event. (The smell of baked goods still hangs lightly in the air.) This morning, the women arrived early to frost and decorate the cookies so that the students could enjoy fresh, homemade sugar cookies, as if they had been to Grandma's house.
>
> "Awesome!"
>
> "Oh wow!"
>
> "Look at all of those cookies!"
>
> "Thank you so much!"
>
> The senior ladies look delighted as the students react to the beautiful cookies. With two or three cookies in hand, the Varsity Choir members scatter around the room and sit at tables with the seniors. Deb addresses the room with a smile.
>
> "Good afternoon, ladies and gentlemen! We are here to make music with you and sing some mushy love songs on this lovely Valentine's Day. Now, the kids are not as familiar with some of these songs as some of you may be, so please feel free to sing loud and proud and teach these classics to the younger people."

"How about ... *(Deb dramatically sings the title of the first song)* 'Love Me Tender.'"

Deb plays an introduction to the first love song on the piano. A small crowd of men at the far end of the room tease Deb and the students about having to stop their poker game as they walk by the cookie table before joining in the singing. The crowd sings through "Tea for Two," "They Can't Take That Away from Me," "Some Enchanted Evening," "You Are My Sunshine," "L-O-V-E," "That's Amore," "Heart and Soul," "Sentimental Journey," and "Hello Young Lovers." Both young and old are smiling, laughing, and singing. The intern teacher takes many pictures of students and seniors as they interact and enjoy the sugar cookies.

During a break, Deb approaches her long-time friend, Bill, who is seated at a table by himself. Bill smiles at Deb with sadness in his eyes. Bill's wife of 50 years, Gladys, passed away in November. Deb, having been at Gladys's funeral, recognizes that Bill is hurting. Waving over some of her "safe girls," Deb introduces the students to her friend. "Girls, I want you to meet my sweet boy, Bill. He needs some music over here and we are not about to let him sit alone on Valentine's Day!" The girls smile, "Hello!" and sit at the table with Bill. Emily shares her word sheets with Bill and he sings softly with the students. The girls are unaware of Bill's sadness and Deb watches him smile at the giggly girls.

Before the final song of the day, a senior woman named Mary stands up at her seat. "You know Ruth and Ollie," she says, gesturing to the couple sitting next to her at the table. "They won't tell you this, but they met here at the Senior Center and they're getting married in August!" The room explodes into a round of applause, cheers, and an "Awww" from the students. Ruth and Ollie cuddle against each other, smiling, sharing a pink word sheet. Ruth's cheeks turn as pink as her sweater and Ollie smiles a broad smile from underneath his dome hat.

"What wonderful news! Congratulations!" Deb smiles broadly, "And what a wonderful time to sing our last song that just happens to be 'Goin' to the Chapel!' This is so cool! We expect you to sing extra loud, Ruth and Ollie!" Everyone in the room laughs and Ruth blushes even more. One more fancy piano introduction and the crowd breaks out into song. People sway from side to side, bouncing their heads with the beat of the music.

"Goin' to the chapel and we're ... gonna get ma-a-arried. ..."

As the caroling draws to a close Deb addresses the crowd: "Remember, we'll be back in May for Memorial Day caroling. It will be all patriotic songs then. Thank you so much for having us! The cookies were such a special treat! You all take care, see you in May, and Happy Valentine's Day!"

At Kinawa Middle School the following day, photographs from Valentine caroling have been arranged on two large pieces of poster board and are on display in the choir room. Deb begins each class period by drawing attention to the photographs. She points out Bill, the widower, who is smiling in the picture with the Varsity Choir students.

"I didn't get a chance to see you after our trip, but I wanted to tell you about one man. And what you didn't know about Bill yesterday is that. . . ." Deb tells her students about the death of Bill's wife, Gladys. The students listen to Deb in respectful silence. Several of the students offer a soft "That's so sad" as Deb tells Bill's story. "And so yesterday was his first Valentine's Day without the love of his life. So while we were there singing gooshy mushy ridiculous love songs, he was sitting there feeling like his heart was being ripped out of his chest because of not being with Gladys. And you did something very, very cool for him. Many of you were standing near Bill when I was over lovin' him up a little bit and so a number of you also had a chance to be near Bill."

Deb's reflection on the caroling turns to Ruth and Ollie and their approaching wedding. Again, many students "Awww" and "Ohhh." "They were sitting in the front sharing a pink word sheet! How darn cute could they be? It was so lovely to be singing them towards a wedding with 'Goin' to the Chapel of Love' and then to heal Bill with your love. It was rather special. Thank you."

Research conducted by Kendall Cotton Bronk (2008) examined early adolescents' conceptions of what it means to have a good life and to be a good person. All but one of her interviewed participants (twelve sixth-graders and thirteen ninth-graders) said that being a good person involved treating others well, which included being nice, being honest or authentic, not judging others, being thankful, putting others first, helping others, caring for others, being polite, being loyal, being respectful, and not harming others. As can be imagined, Deb's endorsement of random acts of kindness has encouraged many of her choir students to demonstrate some of these characteristics outlined by Bronk, as evidenced by the following conversation with a small group of Deb's students:

LUKE: She's really into the "random acts of kindness" thing. At least one day every week she'll read out of this little *Random Acts of Kindness* book and they're examples of people that. . . . *(All the boys start talking at once.)*

CHRIS: How you can be nice and stuff. Short stories about it, too.

JASON: People who, like, give horses to their friends for no good reason and like. . . .

CHRIS: Clean the lady's car who lives down the street who couldn't do it. . . .

BRIDGET: She reads once a week?

JASON: It's not on a schedule. It's whenever she feels like it.

LUKE: Like if we have time at the end of class or something.

BRIDGET: How do people respond when she does that?

CHRIS: We are in awe by some of the things that have been said and done. *(The boys are saying "Yeah" and "Yes" to agree with comments expressed.)*

JASON: It's pretty cool!

LUKE: And we react well. We'll do it. We'll do random acts of kindness. Like there was one time, Little Debbie. . . . *(The other boys say "Oh yeah" with a serious tone.)*

TONY: That was so sad.

CHRIS: Mrs. Borton's niece passed away due to an illness.

JASON: Heart defect, I think. She had a staph infection or something. *("Yeah.")* And her immune system was so weak. *("Yeah.")*

CHRIS: She was, I think, cognitively impaired. She was twenty-two. I heard that someone in her school called her a "retard" so she went home and she asked Big Debbie (that's Mrs. Borton), "Am I really retarded?" Mrs. B was like, "No, the person who called you 'retarded' would be the one who is actually the stupid one." To realize it's what's inside a person as opposed to *how* they act and stuff and that was just downright wrong and mean of them.

TONY: Following Little Debbie's death, people made signs that said, "We love Little Debbie" and stuff in memory of her.

LUKE: We made shirts and stuff. *(Lots of talking at the same time about what students did for Mrs. Borton during this time.)* We hung signs up on Mrs. Borton's door. Yeah, it was pretty sad.

CHRIS: So we all pitched in and signed cards and did things.

BRIDGET: I bet that meant *a lot* to her.

JASON: Yeah. *("Yeah, it did.")*

CHRIS: The whole choir works as a *group* opposed to being all individuals trying to sing our own parts and that's not all. It's inside choir and outside choir. *(Several boys say "Yeah.")* All around the school, we're always tryin' to help someone else.

BRIDGET: Why do you think that is?

CHRIS: I guess it is Mrs. Borton's impact on us.

JASON: It's just sort of the whole *experience*; we've all sort of shared something.

CHRIS: It's like a chain reaction. Like Jason said, we all share something. . . .

JASON: We all shared something that's so powerful and . . . *different* that it kind of makes us work together and be. . . .

CHRIS: Who we are, who we are.

I was living in Chicago and going through what was a particularly cold winter both in my personal life and the outside temperature. One evening I was walking home from a bar where I had been drinking alone, feeling sorry for myself, when I saw a homeless man standing over an exhaust grate in front of a department store. He was wearing a filthy sport coat and approaching everyone who passed by for money. I was too immersed in my own troubles to deal with him so I crossed the street. As I went by, I looked over and saw a businessman come out of the store and pull a ski parka out of a bag and hand it to the homeless man. For a moment both the man and I were frozen in time as the businessman turned and walked away. Then the man looked across the street at me. He shook his head slowly and I knew he was crying. It was the last time I have ever been able to disappear into my own sorrow. (*Random Acts of Kindness* 2013, 66)

EMPATHY

Empathy is vital if children are to join the community of others with all the skills and virtues that define our species at its best. With empathy, we can love, listen, understand and imagine. We can work together, share, and create. We can tolerate, forgive, show mercy, apologize, repair, and hope. We know what empathy is. We know how it can be nurtured. We just need the will to continue finding the way to do so. (D. Howe 2013, 202)

Comments above from Deb's students not only demonstrate the students' developing awareness of others but also a developing sense of empathy for others. "Empathy lets all kinds of emotions reverberate amongst us. It is the capacity to recognize and identify with what another person is thinking or feeling, and to *react* with a comparable emotional state" (Frazzetto 2013, 148). Robert B. Brooks has written extensively about child resilience, motivation, and family relationships. In his chapter "Creating a Positive School Climate," he frames his discussion of empathy specifically within the adolescent classroom and starts with some very frank and truthful statements worthy of contemplation for *us* as music teachers.

Typically, it is most difficult to be empathetic toward those students who challenge us, who question our authority, who fail to do their homework, who act up in class. Yet, it is precisely with these students that we must expend much energy to be empathic. Unless we understand the developmental issues of middle school children, unless we have a sense of what their words and actions represent, unless we appreciate both the middle school child's anxieties about growing up and the child's strong quest for separation and independence (a quest often expressed in ways that push adults aside and even seem to belittle adult values), it can become easy to lock horns with them and respond to them in negative ways. (Brooks 1999, 63)

Without *our* first taking steps toward empathy for others as music teachers, we cannot expect our students to consider such strides on their own. It really begins with us teaching our students about the importance of empathy for others and how it allows us to "recognize our own hopes and fears as we listen to others talk of their hopes and fears. To lose our empathy would be to lose our humanity" (D. Howe 2013, 198). Robyn (strings) shared a story about one of her students during our interview and became quite emotional as she expressed great empathy for this person.

ROBYN: I had a student who had a very tragic situation happen and he was just checked out. And in (oh my God, I could cry thinking about it) but coming into orchestra was a way for him to escape what was going on, and so he would hang around—(*growing more emotional*) oh my God—he would hang around after orchestra, just like hang around. And I said to him, "Hey, how's it going?" And he's like, "Oh, you know, it's good." And he would kind of stand around. He started to ask, "Can I help you with anything?" "Oh no, I'm good." But when I realized that he wants to stay and wants to still be here. . . .I didn't need help pushing my cart back to my office but, "Hey do you want help push this cart back? I could use some extra help." He was just so grateful to do that. I look at my own personal experience and in high school I was so close with my orchestra director—because I had a lot of things going on in high school—and my orchestra director (*continually more emotional*) oh my gosh—was always there for me. And so I wanted (*voice cracks*) . . . why am I like this?! (*begins to cry*)

BRIDGET: You're emotional because you care so much, which makes you such a great teacher. It's not a bad thing. It's not a bad thing at all. It's a really cool thing.

ROBYN: Orchestra teachers cry. That's what you can write in your book. (*chuckles*)

BRIDGET: That speaks so much of your character. You do recognize that, don't you?

ROBYN: Yeah. Well . . . thanks.

Steve Springer and Kimberly Persiana wrote in *The Organized Teacher's Guide to Classroom Management*, "Give a student the benefit of the doubt whenever you can. Empathy on your part can go a long way. You may be the only person who recognizes the good in that student. In certain situations, you may be all a particular student has" (Springer and Persiani 2011, 100). Empathy does not equal liking—you don't have to like someone to be empathetic with him or her. However, "empathy requires respect for people different from ourselves. Our respect for them causes us to be open-minded, to carefully consider their views when those views are different from ours" (Wiggins and McTighe 2006, 99). In Deb's classroom, she works to connect with students and validate their feelings on a variety of levels by sharing stories and details from her life to let students know that she is a "real live person and not just a teacher."

DEB: And I'll say "I'm part of a divorced home." And the kids say, "Oh geez. Well I am too." And I say, "I am so sorry for you. That just bites doesn't it? I'm so sorry you are part of a divorced home." So they hear that it's okay. I tell them about my niece, sick and dying and about her being called a "retard"—she was severely disabled in multiple ways—so the kids know about my life and it just gives me credibility.

Some of the other music teachers also shared stories about their efforts toward empathy with their own students. Andrew's (strings) mother passed away near his eighteenth birthday; she was a teacher at his high school and a very beloved person for many reasons.

ANDREW: Hopefully I can be somewhat of a role model to these kids in this way or that. The memory of my mother passing away is pretty—it's still pretty strong. At my graduation there was a moment of silence for my mom. You know being a parent is something very important, but being a teacher can be almost just as important for a lot of these kids.

The death of his mother has greatly influenced Andrew's work and desire to help students, especially those from single-parent homes, by providing them with a sense of love and belonging in his classroom. As part of his efforts, he goes to special lengths to make members of his music program feel special, particularly in times of challenge.

> ANDREW: In my class we throw surprise parties to honor students for their contributions and to let them know how much we love them. For instance, this year a student underwent some invasive back procedures to align his spine and help him grow. He was so scared that wearing a back brace would cause him to be further ridiculed or made fun of; he was already a bit of an awkward kid. He waited until the class departed from the party and let the bell ring to come tell me through tears that he had never felt so loved or so admired by his classmates. You know this is what learning music is about to me; it's about being human and rising well above our perceived limits to share the joys and sorrows around me with these kids.

Marsha (band) is quite open with her students about her own disability in hopes that, because it is a part of who she is (in addition to being a very beloved teacher), her having a disability positively influences the way that her students perceive other people: "I hope that practicing the idea of treating everybody with respect and having a teacher with a disability who loves them and cares about them, it makes them more open to everything about other people."

Seth (choir) has found that experiences of empathy have helped his adolescent singers develop confidence in their musical abilities by increasing their capacity to express emotion, especially through performance. For example, his select ensemble performs at an annual memorial service for loved ones and "that is *gut-wrenching* for them." Inevitably, the singers are all very moved by the stories shared about those who have passed away and cry a great deal during the service. However, the singers close the service by performing a song, which could be challenging for anyone in such an emotional situation. "If you can do *that* concert, you can do anything," Seth says. "Most middle school teachers don't *expect* that students can handle emotion like that; the perception is that they can't feel deeply, but I think that they can."

The quote, "With great power comes great responsibility," was first coined by Voltaire (although more people tend to know this from the recent *Spiderman* movies). This powerful quote holds quite true for us as music educators because (1) we work in positions where we can be incredibly influential to our adolescent music students in a number of ways; and (2) we work with a population in the midst of self-development, who are also significantly open to influences that can help them determine how to live their lives. That's the "great power" piece; next comes the "responsibility" piece.

Whether or not you see yourself in the teacher stories of this chapter, it is important to contemplate how you currently use your influence with adolescents in your music classroom and consider how you could be even more of a positive influence on them through your work as a music teacher and by being a good person. As Michelle (choir) says to her students:

> MICHELLE: You have a gift of music. It is your responsibility as a singer to share that gift. It is your responsibility. When someone calls you and says, "My mom just died. Will you please sing at the funeral?" You *have* to do it. When someone asks you to sing in a wedding, you *have* to do it. They want *you* to be part of that wonderful day or that . . . to get them through a painful time. It's your responsibility.

Therefore, it truly is your responsibility to share your gift of being a thoughtful and caring human being *and* music teacher with other people, especially your own adolescent music students.

> I did not go through my teenage years gracefully. I was overweight and pear-shaped with glasses, braces, and acne. My self-consciousness was aggravated by my little sister who was ten years younger than me and so pretty. She had apple cheeks and long auburn ringlets, and people would stop us on the street just to admire her. One day one of my mother's friends, whom I adored because she was so sophisticated and stylish and because she always treated me as a person rather than a child, complimented me on my eyebrows. She told me that they were so dark and beautifully shaped that they made me look very exotic. Forty years later that single compliment—given so freely and sincerely to a child who did not feel at all attractive or exotic—still fills my heart with gratitude. (*Random Acts of Kindness* 2013, 196)

DIGEST

> You never really understand a person until you consider things from his point of view . . . until you climb into his skin and walk around in it. (Atticus Finch, *To Kill a Mockingbird* [Lee, 1960])

Within the realm of brain research, scientists believe that the right temporal parietal junction (RTPJ) is particularly important for developing empathy. However, scientists are also finding that adolescents may not be using their RTPJ as much as they could because of the amount of time they spend communicating through digital devices, text messages, or social networks.

While scientists are still figuring out how relationships built through technology compare to personal interaction, most believe that person-to-person connection is essential for adolescents to learn effective and appropriate ways of interacting in the world. This is true in other species as well: when contact with other rodents is restricted, even these small creatures fail to develop normal social interactions. These effects are particularly pronounced when social interaction is restricted during adolescence, suggesting that this is a critical/sensitive period for social interaction. You can improve your own chances for healthy social interaction as an adult by ensuring that your interactions with others are not limited to just electronic means such as texting or emailing. (Deak and Deak 2013, 45)

As music educators, we are in prime positions to encourage person-to-person empathic communication between our adolescent musicians. This may come in the form of an actual conversation, such as small- or large-group discussions about musicians, readings, recordings, concerts, compositions, collaborative projects; providing thoughtful and constructive feedback to peers about a performance or work-in-progress; or through musical "conversations" via improvisation, call-and-response activities, musical performances, composition workshops, jam sessions, and so forth. Therefore, this digest section for chapter 5 will focus on a few strategies that may assist your work with adolescents toward developing a greater sense of empathy for others, deepening students' understanding of their place in this world, and heightening their experiences with music as emotions intensify during adolescence. The majority of these strategies come from areas outside of music education, but each would be easily adapted to an adolescent music class setting.

The research study "Adolescent Purpose Development: Exploring Empathy, Discovering Roles, Shifting Priorities, and Creating Pathways" was conducted as part of the Youth Purpose Project at the Stanford Center on Adolescence and revealed that early adolescent years are a prime time for empathy development. According to the researchers, family members greatly influenced adolescent participants' empathetic awareness,

One participant said that his parents discussed environmental impact when they saw a car emitting exhaust, and talked about the beneficiaries of their donations when they contributed to a charity. Angela said that her family taught her, "If you would be able to help other people, then maybe it'll be a better world and a better life." She described watching her mother act on this belief by volunteering for youth programs and said that her mother invited Angela to volunteer with her. (Malin et al. 2013, 192)

However, it was also found that as adolescents began to shift from being family-influenced to peer-influenced, their peers had a negative influence on their sense of purpose to do something in the spirit of empathy. In addition, "few early adolescents described having structured opportunities to act on their empathic concerns, and consequently, their pro-social intentions drifted away when other interest arose" (ibid., 195).

Implications of this research on our work as music educators and advocates of empathic concern are clear: as students navigate through adolescence, we must (1) provide multiple music opportunities for our adolescent music students to think and act in the spirit of empathy (both within and outside of our music classes), as they may not be presented with opportunities on their own; and (2) the provided opportunities should somehow be socially oriented if we wish to counteract negative influence that peers might use to sway adolescents away from involvement in such efforts. The bottom line is that if our music students are *all* taking part in empathic acts alongside their peers and friends, chances are that the experiences will be more meaningful and valuable, and it is less likely that negative influences will abound after such experiences. Examples from this chapter include the students' shared discussions of *Random Acts of Kindness* in music class, promotion of the idea that Singing Produces Awesome Miracles (and doing good for others), and Deb's students' singing with seniors at the Valentine caroling event.

Many resources for promoting empathy in the classroom are available from various organizations online, such as Teaching Tolerance, a project of the Southern Poverty Law Center (www. tolerance.org). The Teaching Tolerance mission is to provide "a place for educators to find thought-provoking news, conversation and support for those who care about diversity, equal opportunity and respect for differences in schools." The following discussion prompts come from a collection of activities put forth by the Teaching Tolerance project to encourage middle school students to understand and practice empathy (http://www.tolerance.org/supplement/developing-empathy-middle-grades). I created music-related adaptations of each original prompt and included those below within brackets:

- One way you can try to imagine what it feels like being in someone else's shoes is to ask yourself, "How would I feel in this situation?" How else can you try to understand how others feel? [Music-related: How do you think the composer felt when writing this piece of music? What do you feel when studying or performing this piece of music? In what ways do you understand what the composer was feeling?]
- When you listen to others, making eye contact, not interrupting the speaker, and asking follow-up questions can show that you're making a genuine effort to understand what they're going through. What other behaviors might show someone that you are being an empathetic

listener? [Music-related: When your peers perform their original songs, what behaviors might show the songwriter that you are being an empathetic listener? What sorts of questions or comments afterward would indicate that you are making a genuine effort to understand his or her perspective during the performance of the song?]

- What can you do to be more attuned to other people's feelings? For instance, when you talk to your friends, how many "you" questions do you ask compared to the number of "I" statements you make? [Music-related: When you talk with your friends about the music they listen to, how many questions do you ask about their musical perspective versus the number of times you talk about your own musical likes and dislikes?] (http://www.tolerance.org/supplement/developing-empathy-middle-grades, accessed September 15, 2015)

Following the above contemplations, Teaching Tolerance encourages students to practice being empathetic by engaging in an activity called "Someone Else's Shoes," which involves twelve different scenarios to which students respond (either to a classmate or through small group discussion) (http://www.tolerance.org/sites/default/files/general/someone%20else's%20shoes.pdf). Official instructions are to "Take one character card, pair up with a classmate, and read your card aloud while your partner practices being an empathetic listener. Then, switch roles: practice being empathetic as your partner, as his character, tells you what he is experiencing." Here are four of the twelve provided scenarios (just for the sake of time and space), each of which could easily be translated into a musical context. Again, I created music-related adaptations and have included them within brackets below:

- During a school field trip, Juan had a seizure in front of his entire class. He came out of it to find all his classmates staring at him. His doctors told him he has a condition where he could have a seizure anytime. [Music-related: This could happen during a music trip, while at a festival, during a musical performance, or during an audition.]
- After practicing for months, Kelsey tripped and fell during her routine for the school talent show. One of her classmates, who was using a cellphone to videotape the show, posted the clip of Kelsey's fall on the Internet the next day. [Although fairly music-related already, this could also be framed within the situation of making a mistake during a concert solo, having one's voice crack severely during a choir concert, or tripping on stage while walking up the choral risers.]
- All of Violet's friends are constantly talking about the prom—the dresses they're going to buy, how they're going to do their hair, where they're

going to eat. Violet wants to go, but the tickets are expensive, and her mom just lost her job. [Music-related: Anything that costs money, including trips, concerts, choir uniforms, involvement in a community music group that requires a fee, participation in a summer music camp, and onward. There are many, many music examples that could work here.]

• Bali found out that a nasty rumor being spread about her was started by a former friend. [Music-related: This one works as is, regardless of setting or context. Unfortunately, this scenario can be common in most populations of adolescents, which is why discussing it is so important.] (http://www.tolerance.org/sites/default/files/general/someone%20 else's%20shoes.pdf, accessed September 15, 2015)

For The Origins Program: Education for Equity (www.originsonline. org), Scott Tyink compiled a list of activities specifically designed to promote and build empathy with adolescents. His list is prefaced by the following comments:

> For middle school teachers, increasing students' capacity for empathy is complicated by the fact that most young adolescents experience an extended "inward" period of development, in which individual identity is an important—at times, paramount—focus. Often lost in the storm of adolescent social-emotional growth, students don't think much about how others feel. How can we help our middle schoolers navigate through this self-centered storm toward a more empathic way of being? Here are some practical ideas to try. (Tyink, 2008).

As you read through Tyink's list, consider how each might manifest in your own adolescent music classroom. What are the short- and long-term ramifications of such efforts with your students? What are the benefits for you, the music teacher, as well as for your classroom environment? (Please note that I have not provided specific music adaptations of these specific activities; everything that follows is as Tyink designed.) Beyond this list, you can find additional resources to use in the promotion of empathy with adolescent music students in the Resources section at the back of this book.

1a. Acknowledgments

Notice empathetic behavior when it happens. Too often, we notice and respond to rule-breaking behavior but forget to acknowledge the good things that happen. Be on the lookout for empathetic behavior, and honor it in a public way when you see it. For example, when Shelly's pen runs out of ink and Larry lends her one of his, mention it: "Larry, you loaned Shelly a pen, so we'll all be able to continue our writing assignment. Thanks!" Or, you could bring your school's group agreements (Social Contract) into the equation: "One of the rules in our Social Contract says, support others. Thanks for honoring our agreements, Larry." (Tyink, 2008)

1b. Ideas for Closing Activities

Popcorn: anyone calls out an acknowledgment to anyone else, without raising hands or taking turns. This version takes away some of the embarrassment in giving and receiving an acknowledgment by deemphasizing each particular compliment. It generates a general feeling of well-being in the group.

Written acknowledgments: students describe in writing times when they saw other students acting with empathy.

Acts of kindness: students acknowledge each other for actions of empathy they witnessed that day. For example, "Davon was empathetic when he picked up my binder for me after I dropped it." (Tyink, 2008)

2a. The Talk Show Game

Materials: None
How to play: Group students in pairs.

In each pair, one plays the role of a talk show host. The other plays the role of a guest on the show. Present each pair with a scenario that involves empathy or lack of empathy. The goal is for the host to elicit an empathetic response by drawing ideas from the guest about some of the experiences, feelings, and attitudes associated with that scenario. The host interviews the guest for one to two minutes, and then the leader gives a thirty-second warning. After the time expires, call for a break, and invite players to stop, switch roles, and take up a new scenario. The process is repeated: the new roles and topic are used within a one- to two-minute time frame. After both students in each pair have played both roles, give the students a few minutes to reflect with each other about the exercise. Possible scenarios for pairs:

- A student does not do well on a test. (Or a playing test or at solo and ensemble festival)
- A girl who heard some gossip appears upset.

- A rumor about you is spreading around the school.
- You were in a fight with your best friend at lunch today.
- You liked your new shoes when you put them on this morning, but somebody made fun of them.
- You thought you would make the basketball team, but you got cut. (Tyink, 2008)

2b. Plan for Success

It is the guest who is practicing empathy by imagining himself or herself in the specific situation and trying to identify what it would feel like. The host should not give advice, but should try to ask questions that assist the guest in getting in touch with what it might be like to be involved in the given scenario. Hosts can ask questions that probe the details of a feeling.

Note: Because this is a challenging line of questioning, in the beginning interviews will likely be short, composed of perhaps four or five questions. As students' skills grow, extend the questioning period. Encourage the hosts not to use "why" questions during the interview process. Often when we ask others to explain why they feel a certain way, we are asking them to rationalize a nonrational experience. This can be confusing and may not forward the empathic experience. Provide specific scenarios, not abstract generalizations. Before playing, model the game with a student, and ask the rest of the class to watch and listen carefully. Play the role of the host, and model asking questions that clarify what the scenario is and lead the guest to his or her own understanding of what someone might feel in this situation. (Tyink, 2008)

An Interview Example:

SCENARIO: a student does not do well on a test.
HOST: How do you feel about your grade on the test?
GUEST: I am disappointed and mad at myself.
HOST: What grade did you hope to receive?
GUEST: At least a C.
HOST: How does it feel when you're mad? What happens inside you?
GUEST: I get tense and crabby. Right now, I can't think about anything but that test.
HOST: Have you felt this way before?
GUEST: Yes—every time I get a bad grade.
HOST: What do you say to yourself or think about yourself? (Tyink, 2008)

3a. Empathic Language

The language of empathy moves away from making judgments and toward describing things accurately. Here is another exercise in which students take on roles and respond from different viewpoints to given social scenarios.

Tell the students that you will leave the classroom and then come back. Their job is to closely observe your behavior. Leave, then walk back into the classroom and make several mistakes in the process: talk loudly, eat some food without permission, take somebody's pencil without asking, and so forth. Tell students to write down on a notecard what they noticed. Collect the cards, and read them aloud. As students listen, ask them to signal one way when they hear descriptive language and another way when they hear judgmental language. Follow this by providing a quick definition: empathetic language is descriptive, not judgmental. (Tyink, 2008)

3b. Four Steps of Empathetic Language

Teach students the following sequence of descriptive, nonjudgmental (empathetic) language:

1. I saw . . . (describe what happened)
2. I felt . . .(describe how you felt when you saw what you saw)
3. I need . . . (describe what you need/would like)
4. I request . . .(make a request for the future)

Example of using the four steps:

1. "You didn't invite me to your party." (statement is a description, not a judgment)
2. "I felt upset. I thought we were friends."
3. "I need to know if you're mad at me."
4. "Next time, will you let me know when you're mad?"

The fourth step is especially challenging because it requires students to identify and express a need through a specific request. Initially, teachers may decide to leave it out. On the other hand, it models ideal behavior, even though it may seem unlikely that students will be able to achieve that level of civility at this time. (These ideas come from American psychologist Marshall Rosenberg; see his book *Nonviolent Communication* for more information.) (Tyink, 2008)

3c. Practicing

Use drama scenarios to practice the language of empathy in social situations students are likely to encounter. Describe the situation (do not act out the negative behaviors) and then have students try it using the four steps of empathetic language in response to the situation (this is the part to act out). You can use the following ideas or provide your own examples, and then ask students to brainstorm a list of scenarios.

- One student is left out of a soccer game at recess.
- Two girls are gossiping about a third girl as she unexpectedly passes, overhearing them.
- A student is repeatedly asked to share his homework with friends, even though the work is supposed to be done independently.
- A student is being pressured to join a gang.
- A boy with poor social skills tends to ostracize himself from the group with awkward, annoying, or slightly antisocial behavior. The group wants to help, but isn't sure how. (Tyink, 2008)

4. Simple musical performances

Musician, author, and cognitive psychologist Daniel Levitin (quite famous for his book *This Is Your Brain on Music: The Science of a Human Obsession*) believes that performing music together is one of the best ways to build people's capacity for empathy. The act itself demands caring relations among the players as well as other empathetic behaviors, such as listening to others, taking turns in the spotlight, playing a supportive role, paying attention to dynamics, and being prepared. Consider the following possibilities:

- Rhythmic call-and-response exercises can be done as energizers or closing activities throughout the day. In a circle, let each student do what she can within four beats; the audience repeats each person's rhythm back to her before the next student shares his.
- Rhythms can be added, one at a time (each student repeating his four-beat phrase, again and again), creating layers of rhythmic complexity. Start by having one student lay down a simple, even, four-beat phrase, either vocally or by snapping fingers, or clapping, or a combination. The second student adds hers as the first student begins a new four-beat phrase, and so on, until each student is contributing to the sound.

When each student starts, he/she must continue his/her phrase, supporting those who follow, and must not change until everyone has joined in.
- Singing rounds is a great way to build empathy through music. Start with simple songs everyone knows. Be sure to lead the group by cueing each section, and by keeping the tempo for the group. (Tyink, 2008)

5. Sharing in the Circle of Power and Respect

Sharing during class can be a great time to build empathy. Try whip shares, where each person in the circle gives a one-word response to a question. Afterward, invite students to ask follow-up questions. With the right topic, the empathy in your room will be palpable! Examples of whip-share topics that can build empathy:

> A pet you've known has passed away
> A painful trip to the dentist's or orthodontist's office
> A time you were ill or hurt
> An experience with baby siblings or other baby relatives
> An experience with puppies, kittens, and other baby animals
> A time when you felt left out
> An embarrassing moment
> Getting cut from a team
> Losing an election

Examples of follow-up questions about a time when you were sick or hurt: "Monroe, how did you get help after you fell?" "Dede, how long were you out of school, and what did you do during that time?" (Tyink, 2008)

6. Buddy classes

Create and maintain a relationship with another class, preferably younger students. There are many activities you can use that facilitate empathetic behavior:

> Read together
> Play board games
> Do a combined class meetings
> Older students plan a party for the younger students

Do a service project together
Do an art project together
Study vocabulary words together

7. Young People's Books

Read and discuss books with explicit themes of empathy, such as:

The Other Side by Jacqueline Woodson
Smokey Night by Eve Bunting
Uncle Jed's Barbershop by Margaree King-Mitchell
Abuela's Weave by Enrique Sanchez
Chicken Soup for the Teenage Soul by Jack Canfield
      and Mark Victor Hansen
Stellaluna by Jannell Cannon (Tyink, 2008)

Moving forward from this chapter, I would like to share one more moment of commentary from Tyrink's discussion of teaching adolescents about empathy.

Weave these ways of building empathy into the class period on any day, in any week. Some become classroom routines, such as acknowledgments. Others are special activities that work well in advisory, such as practicing empathetic language or playing a game. The idea is to consistently infuse your time with students with opportunities to think about others from a fresh, sympathetic point of view. The payoff for teaching empathy is the creation of school communities strengthened by trust and free from constant strife–the kind of social-emotional climate that translates into higher academic performance for everyone. (2008)

CHAPTER 6

Humor in the Music Classroom

Middle school laughter is like the most contagious, beautiful sound . . . because when they are laughing, when they are joyful, when they're happy—they just light up the whole room. (Kate, *general music*)

Laughter is estimated to be 7 million years old. Like other vocalizations, such as moaning, sighing, and crying, laughing is thought to have preceded speech and, like these vocalizations, it may also have a communicative function. (Vaid 2002, 506)

That old saying, "Don't smile at your students before Christmas," has never worked for me, either as a student or as a music teacher. I want to connect with people immediately and I want them to connect with me. Because adolescents can be so very funny, humor is a natural way to connect with and guide them, to show that you are a real person, and to have a great deal of fun in the music classroom. As adolescents are often consumed with self-consciousness and worry, when you get them to laugh you provide them with a break from all of that. And, truthfully, just hearing our adolescent students laugh does so much good for *us*, the music teachers, for it helps us to not take things so seriously. Adolescent laughter can be a kind of fountain of youth if we let it.

Rod A. Martin discussed benefits of humor in the classroom in his book *The Psychology of Humor:*

Humor in the classroom helps to reduce tension, stress, anxiety, and boredom; enhances student-teacher relationships; makes the classroom less threatening for students; makes learning enjoyable, creating positive attitudes toward learning; stimulates interest in and attention to educational messages; increases comprehension, cognitive retention, and performance; and promotes creativity and divergent thinking. (Martin 2007, 350)

Over the years I have found humor to be a powerful tool in my teaching arsenal, but I do respect it at the same time. Humor has the power to uplift and unite our adolescent music students as well as the power to crush and destroy them. It must be used carefully and wisely; anything potentially hurtful or offensive should be avoided. "Any word, object, or action that violates a person's values, moral principles, or norms of behavior would be offensive" (Veatch 1998, as cited in Berk 2002, 12). So, bottom line: when it doubt, don't say it.

In his book *Humor as an Instructional Defibrillator*, Ronald A. Berk presents a myriad of strategies for using humor in a college classroom, but many of his comments are applicable to music settings with adolescent-aged music students. The excerpt I share below is longer but important as we begin our considerations of using humor when working with adolescents.

Humor that can potentially offend any student is inappropriate in the classroom. Why? Because it can have the following negative effects on a student: tightening up, withdrawal, resentment, anger, tension, anxiety, and turning off/tuning out. After reading down this list, does the word *disconnect* come to mind? These physical and emotional effects can squash a student's motivation or spirit to learn, which results in a loss of spunk. Once you've lost spunk, it's over. More importantly, a single offensive joke can irreparably damage your relationship with the student. In other words, you could lose that student for the entire semester. A student would stop coming to class to avoid the preceding feelings, the risk of a reoccurrence, or a confrontation with the perpetrator (YOU!). What is offensive is not determined by a majority vote of the students. It is an individual issue in many cases because humor is open to individual interpretation. However, your experience should weed out most of the offensive material so these individual cases are rare.

The above negative effects are exactly opposite of the positive effects for using humor in the first place. One primary goal is to *connect*. Non-offensive humor can break down barriers, relax, open up, and reduce tension, stress, and anxiety to create the professor-student connection. In addition, it can grab and maintain the students' attention on learning. Furthermore, offensive humor is inconsistent with some of the characteristics of effective teachers, such as sensitive, caring, understanding, compassionate, and approachable. (Berk 2002, 14; emphasis in original)

This chapter on humor consists of two sections. The first takes a look at adolescents and music teachers as potentially humorous people. The second section addresses the idea of using humor as a teaching tactic in the adolescent music classroom, including the use of sarcasm. I feel somewhat compelled to say something funny here, as we are launching into a conversation about humor. Therefore I shall share one of my favorite jokes, taught to me by a sixth grade choir student: How do you get an old lady to say the f-word? You get another old lady to yell, "*Bingo!*"

And away we go.

HUMOROUS PEOPLE

They [adolescents] find humor in things that I don't see. It's almost like they're seeing a sort of parallel universe. *(chuckles)* They have such strong imaginations and use their imaginations in humorous ways. (David, choir and guitar)

The Adolescent Sense of Humor

Adolescents can be downright hilarious. Anyone who works with this population of music students knows that their humor is one of the reasons we continually come back for more. When I hear about silly happenings, I just find the age group that much more endearing. For example, I was teaching at the middle school and forgot something at home and my husband, Jason, was kind enough to bring it to me before he left for work. As he was walking down the hallway to my choir room, a lone student was walking in his direction headed toward the school office. When they neared each other, the middle school student looked at Jason and suddenly waved both arms over his head, stuck out his tongue, rolled his eyes, made some sort of gargling/alienesque noises at him for about ten seconds, and then continued walking normally down the hallway. Poor Jason, who is not a teacher and does not work with adolescents, just did not know how to react to the incident that was completely unprovoked. I thought it was *hilarious* when he told me about it, upon which he said, "And *that* is why you teach middle school students and I do not." His comment really struck me as I did not find the incident outlandish or out of place, but rather, quite in character with my student population. He was right: because I found such things so amusing, working with adolescent students is a good fit for me.

Oftentimes adolescents do not intend to be funny, but it just ends up that way. This was something repeatedly mentioned by the music teachers whom I interviewed.

TAVIA (BAND): Oh my goodness they're hilarious. They are actually starting to develop a sense of humor that doesn't just involve fart jokes, although we have plenty of those. But really, I think they say and do the funniest things, especially as they're growing into that sense of humor. Sometimes, they do funny things that they don't realize are funny just because they're middle schoolers and they're out of it and they don't know how to be funny.

SETH (CHOIR): Their sense of humor can be hilarious—*accidentally*. As you know, they can say some of the dumbest things you've ever heard that are just *hilarious*.

Case in point: Every day in my classroom, I put a quote on the chalkboard for students to read as they enter. One day I provided a quote by Mark Twain and a student asked me, "Isn't that Shania Twain's husband?" Another day I provided a quote by Louis Armstrong and overheard two students talking about it: "Was he the first man on the moon?" "Ummm ... that was *Neil* Armstrong." "Oh. Never mind." In addition, adolescent students can be outright funny simply through their navigation of adolescence and all that it encompasses.

ROBYN (STRINGS): I mean, I think they're hysterical, but for reasons that they probably don't know because I see so much of myself in them from when I was that age. I think, "Did I really talk like that?" or "Did I really dress that way?" Or they're so concerned about the stupidest things that we *now* think are not a big deal, but to them, "Oh my gosh, this one piece of hair is sticking out. I *have* to go push it back!" or "Did you see Johnny give me a smile across the way?!" It's all of the silly things that they do that cause me to chuckle.

Our adolescent music students also use humor to connect with each other in social ways:

MARSHA (BAND): I think it's funny that they share a sense of humor among each other. At the end of one marching band rehearsal, we were all done and I said, "Alright gang, let's go in," and one student yelled, "We. Are. Farmers!" and the rest of the band responded with, "bum-dum-dum-bum-dum-dum-dum." *(chuckles)* It was just like the Farmers Insurance commercial. And it was also funny that he said, "We are farmers," because it's a really rural town. But it was so funny that they all socially just got on that and responded that way. I don't know if other age groups would have done that or not, but I thought that it was hysterical.

From my own middle school teaching days, I remember my students join-ing forces to lure me out into the cafeteria on my birthday so they could all sing to me. However, the way they got me out there was to come and tell me that my new car had just been hit in the parking lot. I admit that they seemed a bit excited about it at the time, so I had my suspicions about what was really happening, but I played along. They all thought it was *awe-some* that their genius plan had worked. They were so proud of themselves and thought they were so clever, and I found their group efforts absolutely charming.

Two of the contributing music educators commented on their enjoy-ment of teaching adolescent music students *how* to appropriately use humor with other people. Marsha (band) shared a funny story about her father's delight in off-color jokes at home when she was growing up, so she did not think much of telling them, herself, as a young person when she was at school or with friends. She just assumed that everyone shared such humor at home. Now, she uses these experiences to help teach her own students about appropriateness:

> MARSHA (BAND): Sometimes their humor is super funny and I love to watch it and laugh and joke with them. But other times I have to take it like a teacher, as an adult in the situation. I have to take the opportunity to teach them a lesson about how to use your humor in the right situations and what's okay, which is a life skill—because sometimes you just can't tell dirty jokes in front of certain people. *(laughs)*

Jay (choir and composition) enjoys teaching his students about the art of subtle humor: "They want to laugh. They need to. They can laugh at themselves, but the trick is to teach them how without embarrassing them. They are learning boundaries of appropriate humor. They love outrageous humor; they need to learn subtle humor."

In 2010 I published a research study titled "A Case Study: Middle School Boys' Perceptions of Singing and Participation in Choir." I interviewed five of my male eighth grade choral students and, needless to say, they were hilariously silly throughout. (I will share a few of their gems in a moment.) However, one of the findings that emerged during analysis of our conversa-tion was that, not only did the boys use humor to be funny and silly and tease one another, they also used humor as a defense mechanism when they were collectively talking about something that made them uncom-fortable or sad—such as being teased by peers as a result of their ener-getic efforts in choir class. The following comes from this article (the boys selected their own pseudonyms):

The second form of Silliness was Defense-Mechanism Silliness. This was a coping mechanism demonstrated during the discussion of how negatively some peers treated them for singing. The boys spoke seriously and did not interrupt one another; they were very respectful of each other. However, as the discussion became more ominous, the boys injected humor into the conversation to purposely cause a shift in focus to more positive ideas. Defense-mechanism silliness is apparent in the interview excerpt below.

> CLIFF: A lot of kids make fun of people *(other boys say "Yeah" in agreement)* because they think *(sarcastically),* "Oh you're really cool because you sing." If you try, they make fun of you.
> JACK: Even in our class, they make fun of you and the way you sound. And they say that you don't sound good and that you're a teacher's pet. . . .
> CLIFF: [The teacher] was showing us how to get better notes on some song . . . they [other boys in the choir class] just burst out laughing sometimes.
> CORNELIUS: Cause like, some of those people think they're so cool. They make fun of people whose voices haven't totally dropped yet because they have to sing up higher. They make fun of them because they're guys and they say that they sound like girls or little kids, but it's harder than it looks. . . .
> JACK: That they sound like they're gay . . . *(Long pause)*
> CLEMENTINE: I like having a tenor voice! *(Lots of "So do I!" and "Yeahs!")*
> CALEB: Sometimes kids outside of choir make fun of you because they're just . . . it seems like that they just, they . . . *(another long pause in the conversation)*
> CLIFF: But wait! In ten years, when we're making millions of dollars because we're singers, they're gonna be, like, "Give me a ride in your sweet truck or car! Come on, give me money—I'm blind and I have rotted out teeth and I live in that little pizza box over there!" *(Everyone laughs.)*
> JACK: Seriously! We'll remember them when we're all, like, on Broadway or a future musical or something or in the movies or just singing for fun, and getting a lot of money . . . *(The group bursts into conversation and laughter.)*
> CLIFF: Or helping our community! (Sweet 2010, 10)

This finding from my study is worth mentioning because it demonstrates that our adolescent music students are complex creatures even with regard to their use of humor. In addition (and discussed more at length later in this chapter), what adolescents show on the outside does not necessarily reflect what they are feeling on the inside, even within the realm of humor. "Students often have trouble communicating their fears either because they are afraid of being rejected or ridiculed, afraid that they are alone with their problem, or afraid that communicating with others won't help. Humor is often the outlet students choose to communicate their fears about life and death" (Hill 1988, 23). So in our work as music teachers, it is important to maintain a notion of how individual students respond to humor in our classrooms and how they use it with us or with each other.

For your enjoyment, I now share some of the comments made by my eighth grade research participants discussed above. I like to call this grouping of quotes, "The charm of eighth grade boys."

- "I like solos!" "You lick solos?" "I LIKE solos! I LIKE solos!" —Jack and Cliff
- "My goal is to be one of the Charmin guys and to make the best, softest toilet paper. And after eatin' some of that venison chili, right off to the dump!" —Cliff
- "Plus, it's pretty sweet to hear the chicks scream at the concert." —Caleb
- "And now this year I don't want to miss Choraliers [the after-school choir] because I like going to it and having fun. I missed, you know, on Tuesday because I shot a deer, but. . . ." "You shot a tree." "Yeah, sorry." —Cliff and Cornelius
- "If I have some sort of a follow-up question, would it be okay if I were to ask you?" "Can we do one right now?" —Dr. Sweet and Cliff at the conclusion of the interview

The Lighter Side of Adolescent Music Teachers

Many of the teachers whom I interviewed for this book are outright funny people. One of my favorite parts of interviewing them was laughing at all of their stories and things they said. For example, Deb told the story of her first experience taking her sixth graders to a choral festival. She was terrified and ended up singing along with the students during their performance on stage.

DEB: *(laughing)* Whoo-ooo-ooo! The only voice you can hear on the festival CD is *mine!* I sang along the entire performance, both songs! *(both of us laughing loudly)* What a scene, too! Judges' comments: Conductor's not supposed to sing.

BRIDGET: Seriously, they wrote that on your sheet? *(laughing)*

DEB: *(laughing)* Yes! I was *so mortified*, God! I had no idea I was singing, but by God I wanted to make sure they did it right! *(both of us
laughing very hard)* Oh! Oh! *Suckage!* Absolute! Oh! Oh! It was *so*
mortifying! God! I was *so scared!* Yeah, I'm "wet pit city" and it was
just sixth grade choir! Two songs! *(both laughing throughout)* Ooh
man! It was horrible! *Horrible!*

BRIDGET: *(laughing)* I love that you sang with them! That's *fantastic!*

DEB: I did! *(laughing throughout)* You can hear my voice! After festival
I had to tell the students, "We're going to listen to you sing on this
recording but you have to listen *really hard* . . . you're going to hear
a little bit of Mrs. Borton singing too. . . . *(whispering)* Sorry!" *(I'm
laughing nonstop at Deb's caricature of herself)*

BRIDGET: God, that's funny. *(laughing again)*

DEB: So when I say I have a lot to be humble about, *those* are the
things I am talking about. Oh my God, it was so funny. "Director's
not supposed to sing." Okay, sorry. Didn't know!

As a huge fan of *really* cheesy jokes, I enjoyed Marsha's (band) mini standup
comedy session during her interview:

MARSHA: I like middle schoolers because they think that I'm still
funny; they like my corny jokes. Like, How you clean a tuba? With
a tuba toothpaste. A drum set falls off a cliff. Buh-doom-shhhh.
Beethoven's favorite food? *(sing-song)* Banananana! They think that
those are hysterical, whereas I've worked with other age groups
who just didn't get it. But I love it when things get really silent and
I will suddenly say, "A drum set falls off a cliff. Buh-doom-shhhh"
(laughs) and then everyone starts laughing.

There are many more amusing interview moments like these that I could
share, but I shall move forward. However, it is important to mention that
several of the teachers view humor as not only a teaching tactic but also
an essential part of who they are. I understand this, as I feel the same way
about myself. Teacher Bridget and civilian Bridget are very similar people, and humor is very much a part of how both operate. Michelle (choir)
expressed equivalent thoughts:

MICHELLE: Humor is a big part of my teaching, but it is a big part of
who *Michelle* is, too. There's no difference between Michelle and
Ms. B. I mean, who you speak to, that's exactly who I am in the
classroom. There's no difference. I can be serious when I need to

be, but if you choose to associate with me, then you are going to take me for who I am. And I want my students to feel that way about themselves too.

Some of the music teachers were quite matter-of-fact about their perceptions that they were *not* funny people. They acknowledged that, although many music teachers use humor as a shtick to engage adolescents, it just was not for them. So humor can be a valuable tool when working with adolescents, but by all means it does not have to be the "be all, end all" technique for success in the adolescent music classroom. As discussed in previous chapters, it is up to you to decide what works best for *you* within the context of your own classroom, regardless of what other people are doing in theirs.

HUMOR AS A TEACHING TACTIC

> Humor makes everything easier. It makes delivery of instruction easier. It improves the classroom environment. It helps mitigate performance anxiety. It enables risk taking. It's really important but I think it has to be really natural. The best teachers, the people that I really admire greatly, are not people who have memorized some lines, but have allowed their natural pedagogical selves to come out. (David, choir and guitar)

In his article "The Culture of Humour in the Classroom: The Good, the Bad, and the Other," Trevor Strong describes humor as "social gunpowder".

> Humour is inherently neither positive nor negative. It is simply a tool, a different way to communicate. But the laughter and excitement we get from humour disguises its power. Humour is like social gunpowder. Use it the right way and you'll have the class seeing fireworks. Use it the wrong way and it will blow up in your face. Yet somehow, people seem to forget just how dangerous it can be. After all, it seems like so much fun at the time. (Strong 2013, 31)

Strong goes on to discuss three categories of humor in the classroom: the good, the bad, and the other. When humor is "good" it is about building relationships with students and developing a sense of community. In addition, it provides new avenues of communication in your classroom: "If it is something that they want to talk about, but that they are uncomfortable with, they might first approach it with a joke. This can open the door to a more serious conversation" (ibid., 32). When humor is "bad" it can lead to confusion, feelings of belittlement, or shame in students and promote fear in the classroom. The third category of humor is "the other," which focuses on the idea that uses of humor are open to interpretation—whether interpretation by your students, by their parents, or by the school administration. "Everyone has a different version of what is acceptable and, even when you're having fun, you need to ask yourself, 'Could I explain this to a parent? To the principal? To a national news service?'" (ibid., 33).

I present these ideas, not to deter people from wanting to use humor in their music classrooms—that is truly the last thing that I want. But rather, my intention is to provide a framework or lens through which we can closely consider the use of humor in our teaching practices.

Laughing at Ourselves

And I have one of those very loud, stupid laughs. I mean if I ever sat behind myself in a movie or something, I'd probably lean over and tell myself to please shut up. (J. D. Salinger)

As a music educator I have always been okay with poking fun at myself, especially when working with adolescents. I like being the goofy one that everyone can laugh about because it takes some of the pressure off of the music students. Remember how vicious that imaginary audience can be for adolescents? So if they feel that no one is paying attention to them because everyone is snickering at (or with) me, then mission accomplished! In those situations, students are also willing to complete the musical task at hand as a result of this misdirection because there is little or no risk involved at this point. However, I want students to understand that it is okay and safe for everyone to poke a little fun at himself or herself–even for us, the music teachers. "I think you've got to be able to laugh at yourself and your mistakes as a teacher. 'Well that didn't work. So what am I going to do now?' And you have to be able to laugh with the kids at your mistakes" (James, choir). Andrew (strings) and Deb (choir) also share this philosophy.

> ANDREW: I make fun of myself quite frequently in the classroom. I believe it's all right to show vulnerability and to let the students know that it's okay to poke fun at ourselves. I think that's where it has to start, rather than finding other things or experiences to make fun of; it's first important to look at ourselves. I really believe that laughter is the second most important sound in my classroom—the music being the first and my voice maybe a distant third. Having a sense of humor plays into my philosophy of developing awareness in my students—more than anything else. If we can make fun of

ourselves then we're clearly developing a self-awareness that goes well beyond "thinking about our thinking" (as the schools like to encourage us to teach to the students), but to also think about who and why we are and how that affects our actions.

DEB: I like to make kids laugh. And a lot of it is that nobody laughs at me more than me. You know, I am the biggest nerd. My hero is Carol Burnett; she is my all-time favorite. I think she is unbelievable. She just looks so ridiculously stupid and she's just okay with that. I'll never be a classic beauty. No boy is ever going to have a crush on me. Which is not good or bad, it's just, you know, I'm not a physical specimen of absolute beauty. So I try to get 'em with my humor. And they know it's safe for them to not be perfect.

As music teachers, we want our students to be able to laugh at themselves about silly things and to not take themselves so seriously, especially within the realm of music. "If it's getting pretty intense and heavy and serious on a very demanding piece, out of nowhere I'll say, 'What's a pirate's favorite state? Arrrr-kansas.' *(laughing)* So I can use bad jokes like that to keep things at equilibrium to help them realize, whoa—good job, but let's not get too serious at this" (Matthew, band). "When they're frustrated with themselves, if they keep making the same mistake over and over again, I will use humor just to lighten the mood. I feel like the humor takes off the pressure" (Gretchen, strings).

Because adolescent physiological changes can limit or affect the musical abilities of our music students, worries and stress about achieving perfection can send students into a dark spiral of self-criticism and disparaging thoughts—especially if they physically cannot complete a specific task. So encouraging our music students to laugh and acknowledge some lack of personal perfection is a healthy practice for them, and smart for us to encourage. "If you are going to crash, let the whole building hear the landing!" (Deb, choir).

Humorous Interludes

Affect is created when the tendency to respond is inhibited, meaning that our students will experience some sort of emotional reaction when we do something that they do not expect. If we use humor at unexpected times while teaching—if our music students are not 100 percent sure of what is coming—they tend to pay closer attention. So in this way, humor can be an excellent mode of classroom management. "If they don't know what's going to come out of our mouth all the time, they pay attention *(chuckles)*" (Tavia, band).

Using humor in this way is also about teaching our students how to change focus when necessary, which can be a useful skill in music for a variety of reasons. For example, Seth (choir) used small humorous breaks in class to train his choral students to switch emotional gears between different kinds of pieces during performances.

> SETH: I want them to enjoy the class, but I also want them to understand that there is a time and a place for it. And I'll use humor and do something to purposely distract them to teach them to *(snap!)* get their mind back on what they're supposed to be doing. And let's say that they do a sixteenth-century madrigal and the next song is a very contemporary piece; they have to be able to switch moods almost immediately so they have to learn to focus. I use humor in that case to get them *out* of focus and then snap them back in. And that's something that starts *right* from the first day in sixth grade. It also keeps their attention on me.

Humor in small, sporadic amounts can also help us gauge the mood of our students or assess the engagement of our teaching over the course of a class or rehearsal. If students react to our moments of humor differently from our expectation, then the flexibility we allow in our classroom structure permits us to tweak the lesson immediately to better meet our students' needs that day. "I feel like it's a kind of measure of how you're doing. If you're making a joke and they're laughing, you're probably doing a pretty good job" (David, choir and guitar).

Sarcasm

> I would have liked to have finished writing the S.P.A.M. [Singing Produces Awesome Miracles] song by now. I'd also like thinner thighs and more money, but those aren't going to happen. (Deb, choir)

In 2001 Jodi Nelms completed her dissertation, "A Descriptive Analysis of the Uses and Functions of Sarcasm in the Classroom Discourse of Higher Education," through which she examined the use of sarcasm in the college classroom. Nelms reported that sarcasm could take one of three forms in the classroom: positive, negative, or neutral. Each of these forms has a different purpose and is used differently, especially depending upon teacher and context. Read the following excerpt as if it discusses teachers of adolescents and not college professors; I think that you will find the same notions, regardless of either population:

> The most frequent *positive* use of sarcasm from this data was for humorous intent. These instances functioned to build classroom rapport by lightening the atmosphere of the class (e.g., deflecting some type of uncomfortable situation) and sparking interest in the subject matter. Sarcasm also served to lessen the gap between teacher and student in cases of self-denigrating sarcasm, for example. Sarcasm was also used positively when professors were trying to make a point, to push students, to react to minor irritations, and in one case, as an indirect reprimand. (Nelms 2001, 68)
>
> *Negative* functions of sarcasm were realized in several ways: ridiculing the students, scolding the students in the form of an indirect reprimand, pushing the students to perform, and using a sarcastic remark defensively. Sarcasm was also used negatively when a professor was reacting to minor irritations. (ibid., 81)
>
> Certain sarcastic utterances were classified as *neutral* when they did not seem to have either an adverse effect or a positive effect on the students. (ibid., 89)

The music teachers to whom I spoke were very divided on their feelings about using sarcasm with adolescent music students. There was no middle ground—they either embraced it or were against using it. Those who enjoyed sarcasm in their music classes felt that their students understood their sense of humor because of the teacher-student relationship that had been established; humor was delivered and received in a funny and safe way. So with regard to Nelms's research discussed above, the teachers to whom I spoke who incorporated sarcasm into their music classrooms used positive or neutral forms of this variety of humor. This was quite evident to me in all the examples provided; these same teachers were overtly against the use of negative forms of sarcasm.

The music educators who did not use sarcasm were primarily concerned that such comments could be intended or misinterpreted as mean-spirited. Many deemed sarcasm a more adult form of humor and, because young adolescents can still be quite *young*, they may not truly understand what is being said. These teachers felt that the only exception for using sarcasm in the music classroom might be to use it against you, as the teacher.

We work with adolescents who, in their quest to fit in, will laugh at things that they really do not think are funny or will go along with something that they find uncomfortable. In so many ways, our music students just aim to please.

If we are teasing in a way that feels negative, judgmental, or mean, students may act like things are okay, even if they are not, just to give the appearance that all is well. This does not mean that you can never joke around or use sarcasm with your students; however, constant mindfulness and sensitivity are essential to make sure that everyone is truly okay and laughing *with* you.

So, to use or not to use sarcasm? It is not my place to judge or make that call, especially since we are all different people. I admit that I can be a very sarcastic person when the mood strikes, but I would never use negative forms of sarcasm with students, as that goes against my entire philosophy of teaching adolescent musicians and my advocacy for "safe place" in the music classroom. However, in my quest to make people laugh, I do enjoy both positive and neutral forms of sarcasm. The bottom line is that when working with anyone, I always try to read each person as best I can to determine the kind of humor that I *could* use with him or her—if at all. Overall, I have been very successful with my efforts of using humor in positive ways, but my rule is to always err on the side of careful and cautious when I just am not sure.

DIGEST

Humor can be a multifaceted component of the adolescent music classroom and a very effective teaching tool. It is not a go-to tactic for all music teachers, and that is okay. However, when using humor as a teaching tactic, it must be approached and executed mindfully. Humor used for good can engage students in musical experiences, but if used negatively, it may damage relationships and impair students' sense of themselves as people and musicians. Sarcasm should be employed selectively and used only in positive or neutral ways.

As this is the conclusion of a chapter on humor, it seems appropriate to end with some wit. The following is a nod to end-of-the-book discussion questions from B. J. Novak's collection of short stories, *One More Thing: Stories and Other Stories*. Enjoy!

DISCUSSION QUESTIONS

- Did you think the book was funny? Why or why not?
- Did you flip through the book and read the shortest stories first? The author does that, too.
- What is quantum nonlocality? Be concise.

- Do you think discussion questions can be unfairly leading some-
  times? Why?
- Who are we supposed to be discussing these questions with?
- Do you normally have discussions in response to a question that was
  posed by a person not participating in the discussion? Why or why not?
- Do you think "why not?" is ultimately a better question than "why?"
- Why or why not?

(Novak 2014, 272)

RESOURCES

This resource section was compiled with the intention that items or discussion here may enhance or enrich your exploration into topics discussed within this book. The following suggested resources are organized by the chapter that they supplement. Citations for publications discussed within each chapter can be found in the reference section at the back of this book.

CHAPTER 1: THE ADOLESCENT MUSICIAN

A quick Google search will yield a great number of suggestions for additional representations of what life feels like during adolescence. However, in addition to those discussed in chapter one, here are a few suggestions to get you started:

Research-based literature:

- Pipher, M. 1994. *Reviving Ophelia: Saving the Selves of Adolescent Girls.* New York: Riverhead Books.
- Wiseman, R. 2009. *Queen Bees and Wannabees.* 2nd ed. New York: Three Rivers Press.

Additional resources on the adolescent brain:

- Philp, R. 2007. *Engaging 'Tweens and Teens.* Thousand Oaks, CA: Corwin Press.
- Siegel, D. J. 2013. *Brainstorm: The Power and Purpose of the Teenage Brain.* New York: Penguin.

Fictional literature:

- *Wonder* by R. J. Palacio (2012)
- *The Misfits* by James Howe (2003)
- *Diary of a Wimpy Kid* series by Jeff Kinney (began in 2007)
- Later books in the *Harry Potter* series by J. K. Rowland (began in 1999)

Television shows:

- *My So-Called Life* (1994–1995)
- *Boy Meets World* (1993–2000)
- *Freaks and Geeks* (1999–2000)
- *The Wonder Years* (1988–1993)
- *The Goldbergs* (2013–present)
- *Moone Boy* (2012–present)
- *Bunheads* (2012–2013)

Movies:

- *The Breakfast Club* (1985)
- *Stand By Me* (1986)
- *Big* (1988)
- *Welcome to the Dollhouse* (1995)
- *About a Boy* (2002)
- *Mean Girls* (2004)

The book *Adolescence: The Real Deal* by Barbara Sheen is a guidebook intended for adolescents to help them better understand the processes of puberty (Sheen, B. (2008). *Adolescence: The Real Deal*. Chicago: Heinemann Library). Physical and emotional changes are discussed, as are the male and female reproductive systems. In addition, Sheen recommends the following books and websites for information about adolescence:

- Elliot-Wright, S. 2004. *Puberty*. Chicago: Raintree.
- Shaw, V. 1999. *Body Talk: A Girl's Guide to What's Happening to Your Body*. New York: Rosen Publishing Group.
- Silverstein, A., V. Silverstein, and L. Nunn. 2000. *Puberty*. New York: Franklin Watts.
- Tym, K., and P. Worms. 2005. *Coping with Your Emotions*. Chicago: Raintree.
- Kids Health: Growing Up: www.kidshealth.org/kid/grow
- American Academy of Pediatrics: Puberty: www.aap.org/family/puberty.htm
- American Social Health Association: Puberty—a beginner's guide: www.iwanna-know.org/puberty/
- Preteen Health Talk: www.pamf.org/preteen/

In his book *Adolescence* Ian McMahan recommends the following resources for scholarly writings about adolescence:

- *Journal of Adolescent Research, Journal of Early Adolescence, Journal of Research on Adolescence, Journal of Youth and Adolescence,* and *Youth and Society*.
- Journals with a broader focus that publish research on adolescents include *Child Development, Developmental Psychology, Family Relations, Journal of Marriage and the Family,* and *Journal of Personality and Social Psychology*.
- For reference works, consider the *Encyclopedia of Psychology* (Kazden 2000), the *Handbook of Adolescence* (Adams and Berzonsky 2002), and the *Handbook of Adolescent Psychology* (Lerner and Steinberg 2004). Unlike journals, books of this sort do not report on new research; instead, recognized authorities give critical overviews of their particular areas of expertise and summarize the important findings and issues.

For information on adolescent female and male voice change, the following publications may be helpful:

- Abitbol, J., P. Abitbol, and B. Abitbol. 1999. "Sex Hormones and the Female Voice." *Journal of Voice* 13: 424–446.
- Alderson, R. 1979. *Complete Handbook of Voice Training*. West Nyack, NY: Parker.
- Barham, T. J. 2001. *Strategies for Teaching Junior High and Middle School Male Singers: Master Teachers Speak*. Santa Barbara, CA: Santa Barbara Music Publishing.

- Barham, T. J., and D. L. Nelson. 1991. *The Boy's Changing Voice: New Solutions for Today's Choral Teacher*. Miami, FL: Belwin/Warner Bros.
- Barlow, C. A., and D. M. Howard. 2002. "Voice Source Changes of Child and Adolescent Subjects Undergoing Singing Training: A Preliminary Study." *Logopedics Phoniatrics Vocology* 27: 66–7
- Brunssen, K. 2010. "The Evolving Voice: Profound at Every Age." *Choral Journal* 51, no. 1: 45-51.
- Cooksey, J. M. 1977a. "The Development of a Contemporary, Eclectic Theory for the Training and Cultivation of the Junior High School Male Changing Voice: Part I: Existing Theories." *Choral Journal* 18, no. 2: 5–14.
- Cooksey, J. M. 1977b. "The Development of a Contemporary, Eclectic Theory for the Training and Cultivation of the Junior High School Male Changing Voice: Part II: Scientific and Empirical Findings; Some Tentative Solutions." *Choral Journal* 18, no. 3: 5–16.
- Cooksey, J. M. 1977c. "The Development of a Contemporary, Eclectic Theory for the Training and Cultivation of the Junior High School Male Changing Voice: Part III: Developing an Integrated Approach to the Care and Training of the Junior High School Male Changing Voice." *Choral Journal* 18, no. 4: 5–15.
- Cooksey, J. M. 1978. "The Development of a Contemporary, Eclectic Theory for the Training and Cultivation of the Junior High School Male Changing Voice: Part IV: Selecting Music for the Junior High School Male Changing Voice." *Choral Journal* 18, no. 5: 5–17.
- Cooper, I., and K. O. Kuersteiner. 1965. *Teaching Junior High School Music*. Boston, MA: Allyn & Bacon.
- Elorriaga, A. 2011. "The Construction of Male Gender Identity through Choir Singing at a Spanish Secondary School." *International Journal of Music Education* 29: 318–32.
- Freer, P. K. 2009. "'I'll Sing with My Buddies'—Fostering the Possible Selves of Male Choral Singers." *International Journal of Music Education* 27: 341–55.
- Freer, P. K., and MENC [National Association for Music Education (U.S.)]. 2009a. *TIPS: The First Weeks of Middle School Chorus*. Lanham, MD: Rowman & Littlefield Education.
- Freer, P. K., and MENC [National Association for Music Education (U.S.)]. 2009b. *Getting Started with Middle School Chorus*. Lanham, MD: Rowman & Littlefield Education.
- Gackle, L. 1991. "The Adolescent Female Voice: Characteristics of Change and Stages of Development." *Choral Journal* 31, no. 8: 17–25.
- Gackle, L. 2000. "Understanding Voice Transformation in Female Adolescents." In L. Thurman and G. Welch, eds., *Bodymind and Voice: Foundations of Voice Education*, rev. ed., pp. 739–44. Iowa City: National Center for Voice and Speech.
- Gackle, L. 2006. "Finding Ophelia's Voice: The Female Voice during Adolescence." *Choral Journal* 47, no. 5: 28–37.
- Gackle, L. 2011. *Finding Ophelia's Voice, Opening Ophelia's Heart: Nurturing the Adolescent Female Voice*. Dayton, OH: Heritage Music Press.
- Kennedy, M. A. 2002. "'It's Cool Because We Like to Sing': Junior High School Boys' Experience of Choral Music as an Elective." *Research Studies in Music Education* 18: 26–36.
- Kennedy, M. C. 2004. "It's a Metaphorphosis: Guiding the Voice Change at the American Boychoir School." *Journal of Research in Music Education*, 52: 264–280.

- Killian, J. 1997. "Perceptions of the Voice-Change Process: Male Adult versus Adolescent Musicians and Nonmusicians." *Journal of Research in Music Education*, 45: 521–535.
- Killian, J. 1999. "A Description of Vocal Maturation among Fifth- and Sixth- Grade Boys." *Journal of Research in Music Education*, 47: 357-369.
- May, W. V. and Williams, B. B. 1989. "The Girl's Changing Voice." *Update: Applications of Research in Music Education*, 81: 20–23.
- Palant, J. 2014. *Brothers, Sing On!: Conducting the Tenor-Bass Choir*. Milwaukee, WI: Hal Leonard.
- Phillips, K. H. 1992. *Teaching Kids to Sing*. New York, NY: Schirmer Books.
- Rutkowski, J. 1984. "Two Year Results of a Longitudinal Study Investigating the Validity of Cooksey's Theory for Training the Adolescent Male Voice." In M. Runfola, ed., *Research Symposium on the Male Adolescent Voice*, pp. 86–96. Buffalo: State University of New York Press.
- Sweet, B. 2015. "The Adolescent Female Changing Voice: A Phenomenological Investigation." *Journal of Research in Music Education*, 63, no.1: 70–88.
- Weiss, D. 1950. "The Pubertal Change of the Human Voice." *Folia Phoniatrica*, 2: 126–159.

At the end of her book *Growing Up Inside and Out*, Kira Vermond provides the following list of websites (and very helpful annotations) for adolescents looking for additional information in any of the following areas (2013, 96–98):

- Body Changes
  - kidshealth.org/kid/grow
    - Wondering why your body is growing and changing? This web site, offered by Nemours, an American children's health organization, will answer a lot of your questions.
  - pbskids.org/itsmylife/body/puberty/
    - What's puberty and what does it do to your body, brain, and emotions? Well, this book covers all of that and more, but if you still have questions, check out this site from PBS Kids. Bored? Do the puberty crossword puzzle. Seriously. This site has one.
- Self-Esteem and Body Image
  - mediasmarts.ca/body-image/body-image-introduction
    - Learn more about girls, boys, and body image here.
  - about-face.org
    - Don't fall for the media circus! About-Face gives women and girls tools to understand and resist harmful media messages that affect their self-esteem and body image.
- Stress, Emotions, and Depression
  - mindcheck.ca/mood-stress
    - Are you stressed? Take the quiz and find out. Lots of useful information about stress, anxiety, and depression.
  - kidshelpphone.ca/Teens/InfoBooth/Emotional-Health/Depression.aspx
    - If you're feeling stressed and depressed, this site is a good place to find out how you can start to feel better. If you live in Canada, you can call the toll-free line and talk to a real person who can give you some help, too.
  - au.reachout.com/Helping-a-friend-with-depression

- Maybe you're not the one going through depression, but your friend is. Here's a site that can give you tips for helping someone else. It offers information to help you take care of *your* feelings and moods, too.
- Eating Disorders
  - eatright.org/kids
    - Learn how to eat a healthy diet and feel good, too. Scientifically based health and nutrition information is a few clicks away.
  - ChooseMyPlate.gov
    - Track your food with this site and see how your diet measures up.
  - nedic.ca
    - The National Eating Disorder Information Centre in Canada is the place to go for information, statistics, and a checklist to see if you or a friend has an eating disorder.
- Bullying
  - stopbullying.gov
    - The US government's comprehensive site for kids, parents, and teachers. Understand what bullying is and how to stop it—there's even a number to call if you live in the United States and need to talk.
  - netsmartzkids.org
    - Give cyber-bullies the boot with this site and learn how to use the Internet safely.
  - bullying.org
    - Use this site to learn a ton about why kids treat other kids badly and what to do about it.
  - canadiansafeschools.com/students/overview/htm
    - If you're being bullied, you're not alone. The Canadian Safe School Network can help!
- Being Gay
  - pflag.org
    - American organization for parents, families, and friends of lesbians and gays. It has support hotlines, too.
  - pflagcanada.ca
    - Canadian? Here's the super-helpful and supportive site for you.
  - youcanplayproject.org
    - You Can Play Project. Gay athletes. Straight allies. Teaming up for respect.
- Healthy Relationships
  - blog.loveisrespect.org
    - Your friend is dating someone who is controlling, jealous, and suspicious. What should you do? Visit this site for loads of information about how to build healthy relationships and put an end to dating violence and disrespect. Check out the "Power and Control" wheel.
  - plannedparenthood.org/health-topics/birth-control-4211.htm
    - Planned Parenthood is a great resource if you have questions about birth control, relationships, and even body image.
  - whitehouse.gov/1is2many
    - Just say no to dating violence.
- Talk it out!
  - Got problems? Feeling upset and want to talk to someone right now? Many countries around the world offer real-time help for real-life problems that kids

experience every day. For instance, in the United States there's the Boys Town National Hotline (and, yes, girls can use it, too) at 1-800-448-3000. Counselors take calls about depression, suicide, bullying, divorcing parents, and even gang violence. In the UK, kids call ChildLine at 0800 1111. In Canada, if you're younger than twenty, you can call Kids Help Phone at 1-800-668-6868, a toll-free, 24-hour counseling and referral service. The calls are anonymous, so you can say whatever's on your mind. Too shy to talk? Many of these services also let you email questions or even chat over IM and get to-the-minute advice from counselors.

CHAPTER 2: THE MUSIC TEACHER

Within the section "Music Educator Role" of chapter 2, discussion was influenced by the ICE method, a classroom approach presented by Sue Fostaty Young and Robert J. Wilson in *Assessment and Learning: The ICE Approach*. In this approach, ICE stands for Ideas, Connections, and Extensions and represents three different levels of learning growth. The first level, *Ideas*, focuses on the building blocks of learning include facts, definitions, concepts, vocabulary, steps in a process, recall of information, and so forth. These are assessed through tasks that involve students strictly recalling information. The second level, *Connections,* could be either content-level connections or connections that are personal and meaningful.

> Connections at the content level are demonstrated when students are able to articulate relationships among discrete Ideas. When students are able to describe cause-and-effect relationships, articulate the relationship between or among concepts, or when they are able to successfully blend two or more discrete skills into a fluid, efficient movement, they are demonstrating Connections at the content level. Connections at the more personal, meaning-making level are demonstrated when students are able to relate their new learning to what they already know. It is during this phase of personal meaning-making that learning appears to take on a new dimension in that it seems to become more easily retrievable and longer-term than learning at the Ideas level. (Fostaty Young 2005, 5)

The third level of learning growth, *Extensions,* is the creation of new learning from old knowledge. Students may use it in creative new ways, perhaps quite differently from the original learning context.

> Extensions are referred to by some as the AHA! phase of learning and by others as the 'so what?' phase. The 'so what' question is the one that is often left unasked: So, now that you know what you know, what difference does it make to the way you see the world and to what you can do? Students reaching Extensions are able to answer those questions. (ibid., 5–6).

For further information on the ICE approach, you are encouraged to read the following:

- Fostaty Young, S., and Wilson, R. J. 1995. *Assessment and Learning: the ICE approach.* Winnipeg, Manitoba: Portage & Main Press.
- Fostaty Young, S. "Teaching, Learning, and Assessment in Higher Education: Using ICE to Improve Student Learning." *Proceedings of the Improving Student Learning Symposium, London, UK* 13 (September): 105–15.

CHAPTER 3: CULTIVATING MUSIC CLASSROOM CLIMATE

As you consider your classroom environment, the following online resources may provide helpful information and services:

- http://empowerment.unl.edu
- www.braverytips.org
- www.bornthiswayfoundation.org
- GLSEN: Gay Lesbian Straight Education Network
- HRC: Human Rights Campaign
- Safe School Coalition
- Southern Poverty Law Center/Teaching Tolerance
- "The Alliance": Illinois Safe Schools Alliance
- eCISSA: East Central Illinois Safe Schools Alliance
- Sites on Facebook: Empowerment Initiative; Bullying Research Network
- Teaching Tolerance (free magazine to educators)

CHAPTER 4: ESTABLISHING THE FRAMEWORK FOR SUCCESSFUL MUSIC CLASSES

- In his book *Adolescence*, Ian McMahan recommends the Olweus Bullying Prevention Program that includes schoolwide, classroom, individual and community components. More information can be found at: www.clemson.edu/olweus or at http://www.violencepreventionworks.org/public/index.page

CHAPTER 5: THE HUMANITY OF TEACHING MUSIC

As you reflect on discussions of humanity—including mottos (e.g., Singing Produces Awesome Miracles), Random Acts of Kindness, and encouragement of adolescent empathy—the following resources may help to enrich your contemplations.

- Josh Shipp is a motivational speaker whose work is centered on empowering teens to "choose to dominate your world." His book, *The Teen's Guide to World Domination: Advice on Life, Liberty, and the Pursuit of Awesomeness* (New York: St. Martin's Press, 2010), is very much written for an adolescent/teen crowd, but does provide interesting insight on the adolescent view of the world for those of us teaching the target audience.
- Elementary teacher Jessica Toulis wrote the chapter "Teaching Children Empathy" in the book *Educating from the Heart: Theoretical and Practical Approaches to Transforming Education*. Within her chapter she provided the following list of quality choices for children's literature that highlight empathy (2011, 129--30):
  ○ Blume, Judy, *The Pain and the Great One* (Tate, 1984; Latest edition from Atheneum Books for Young Readers, 2014)
  ○ Bunting, Eve, *Riding the Tiger* (Houghton Mifflin Harcourt, 2001)
  ○ Cannon, Janell, *Stellaluna* (Houghton Mifflin Harcourt, 2007)
  ○ Cheng, Andrea, *Grandfather Counts* (Lee & Low Books, 2003)
  ○ Cherry, Lynne, *The Great Kapok Tree* (Harcourt Brace Jovanovich, 1990; Latest edition from First Voyager Books, 2000)
  ○ Coles, Robert, *The Story of Ruby Bridges* (Scholastic Press, 2004; also, Special 50th Anniversary Edition, 2010)
  ○ Daly, Niki, *Once Upon a Time* (Farrar, Straus & Giroux, 2003)
  ○ Danneberg, Julie, *First Day Jitters* (Charlesbridge, 2000)
  ○ DeRolf, Shane, *The Crayon Box That Talked* (Random House, 1997)
  ○ DiCamillo, Kate, *The Miraculous Journey of Edward Tulane* (Candlewick Press, 2009)

- Hiaasen, Carl, *Hoot* (Random House, 2002)
- Hiaasen, Carl, *Flush* (Random House, 2005)
- Lamorisse, Albert, *The Red Balloon* (Doubleday, 1956)
- McKissack, Patricia C., *The Honest-to-Goodness Truth* (Simon & Schuster, 2003)
- Myers, Christopher, *Wings* (Scholastic Press, 2000)
- Paterson, Katherine, *The Bridge to Terabithia* (Harper Collins, 1987)
- San Souci, Robert D., *The Talking Eggs* (Penguin, 1989)
- Spier, Peter, *People* (Doubleday, 1988)
- Van West, Patricia E., *The Crab Man* (Turtle Books, 2001)
- Viorst, Judith, *Alexander and the Terrible, Horrible, No Good, Very Bad Day* (Aladdin Paperbacks, 1987)
- Woodson, Jacqueline, *Visiting Day* (Scholastic Press, 2002)
- Zolotow, Charlotte, *William's Doll* (Harper Collins, 1985)

A few additional resources towards understanding empathy:

Books:

- Palacio, R. J., *Wonder* (Knopf Books for Young Readers, 2012)
- Palacio, R. J., *365 Days of Wonder: Mr. Browne's Book of Precepts* (Knopf Books for Young Readers, 2014)
- Palacio, R. J., *Auggie & Me: Three Wonder Stories* (Knopf Books for Young Readers, 2015)
- Draper, Sharon M., *Out of My Mind* (Atheneum Books for Young Readers, 2012)
- Sachar, Louis, *Holes* (Farrar, Straus & Giroux, 1998) (also a movie based on the book, *Holes*, 2003)
- Philbrick, Rodman, *Freak the Mighty* (Blue Sky Press, 1993) (also a movie based on the book, *The Mighty*, 1998)
- Curtis, Christopher Paul, *Bud, Not Buddy* (Yearling, 1999)
- Spinelli, Jerry, *Stargirl* (2000) and *Love, Stargirl* (2007) (Alfred A. Knopf)

Movies:

- *Akeelah and the Bee* (2006)
- *Freaky Friday* (2003)
- *Mean Girls* (2004)
- *Pay It Forward* (2000)
- *Radio* (2003)
- *Temple Grandin* (2010)
- *Welcome to the Dollhouse* (1995)

CHAPTER 6: HUMOR IN THE MUSIC CLASSROOM

At this time, I hestitate to recommend specific resources for using humor in the music classroom, especially as we each have our own opinion about what is funny and what is not. Prescriptive books on using humor in education tend to feel, well, prescriptive and that goes against the point of using humor with students in the first place. Really, your biggest resource for using humor in the music classroom is *you*. Therefore, as a middle school music educator, you are encouraged to stay in touch with your adolescent self and maintain a sense of humor and levity in the classroom as much as possible; to continue to search for moments of awe and wonder, for you as well as for your students; and to work hard at not taking yourself too seriously. Simply put, be genuine and have fun and your students will follow your lead.

APPENDIX A
Teacher Participant Extended Bios

Information about the contributing music teachers provided in the Preface of this book reflects each teacher's work at the time of his or her interview. This Appendix provides updated and extended biographies of each contributing middle school music teacher.

Deb Borton retired from teaching in 2014. She taught middle school vocal/ choral music for twenty-three of her thirty-four years as a teacher. The majority of her teaching career was in Okemos, Michigan—a small community located right next to East Lansing and Michigan State University. Deb has a Bachelor of Music Education degree from St. Olaf College and has completed graduate work at Michigan State University, Marygrove College, and Vandercook School of Music.

Bethany Cann is taking time off from teaching school-based music to raise her family. She may return to teaching middle school after her children are older, but in the meantime has plans to form a toddler music class and teach private music lessons out of her home.

Robyn Chair (a pseudonym) completed her Master of Music Education degree and continues to teach orchestra at two middle schools and two elementary schools.

Jay Champion has taught at Lost Mountain Middle School in Kennesaw, Georgia since 1998. He is currently the Director of Choral Activities and also teaches general music and electronic music composition. In addition, he is the Associate Director of Music at Holy Spirit Catholic Church in Atlanta. Over the years, his choirs have given invitational performances at the Georgia Music Education Association Conference, Georgia State University, and the University of South Carolina.

Recognized as a leader in the use of technology in the music classroom, Jay has taught professional courses and presented at state and national conventions.

Jay received a Bachelor in Music Education as a voice major and a Bachelor in Music Composition from Louisiana State University in Baton Rouge. He earned his master's degree in Music Education and an Education Specialist Degree at the University of Georgia in Athens.

James Cumings has been teaching choral music at Jackson Northwest Kidder Middle School in Jackson, Michigan since 1999. Prior to this position, he taught two years of elementary music education in Naperville, Illinois. James earned his Bachelor of Music Education at the Wheaton Conservatory of Music in Wheaton, Illinois, and earned his master's degree in Music Education at Central Michigan University.

James has guest conducted the Boy's PowerSing festival in Naperville, Illinois; he has been a sought-after guest clinician and conductor in Michigan; and he currently serves as a faculty member at Blue Lake Fine Arts Camp in Twin Lake, Michigan. James's choirs have consistently received excellent and superior ratings at choral festivals in both performance and intermediate/advanced sight-reading. His choirs have been featured as part of the Michigan Music Conference, Michigan ACDA State Convention, and the Music Education Convocation at Western Michigan University.

Matthew Dethrow has been teaching band since 1996. He earned his undergraduate from DePaul University, a graduate degree from the University of Illinois, and his Master Teaching Certificate from the National Board for Professional Teaching Standards in 2008. Matthew is an active freelance musician and clinician in Chicago. He is a multi-instrumentalist who performs in a variety of settings from commercial recordings to live performance. He is also an active clinician and teacher with a focus on jazz improvisation.As co-Director of bands at Kennedy Junior High, Mr. Dethrow co-conducts Kennedy Winds and Wind Ensemble. These two bands service the 7th and 8th grade students. He also co-conducts the 6th grade Concert Band and the Jazz Band.

Jason Freeland received his Bachelor of Music Education degree from DePaul University in Chicago and holds a master's degree in school administration. He is the director of bands at Central Middle School (CMS) in Tinley Park, Illinois. Under his direction, the CMS Symphonic and Concert Bands have consistently received division one ratings at the Illinois Grade School Music Association Organization Band Contest. In 2014, the CMS

Symphonic Band was awarded the honor of Grand Champion at Illinois State University's State of Illinois Invitational Contest and was also awarded first place at the prestigious Illinois SuperState Band Festival where the band was recognized as the Honor Band of 2015.

In 2011 Jason received the Chicagoland Outstanding Music Educator Award from Quinlan & Fabish, and was nominated for a Golden Apple Award in 2012 and a Music Educators Grammy Award in 2013.

Seth Gardner retired from teaching classroom and choral music at Haverford Township Middle School in Havertown, Pennsylvania, after thirty-five years of teaching. Prior to arriving in Haverford, he taught choral, band, and instrumental music at junior and senior high school levels at Lackawanna Trail Junior/Senior High School in Factoryville, Pennsylvania. Seth was a string bass major at Ithaca College, graduating in 1975 with a Bachelor of Music degree. He took graduate courses with a choral emphasis at Ithaca College, West Chester University, and Villanova University.

Seth has extensive instrumental performing experience for Broadway musicals and also as the bassist/vocalist for the commercial bands Easy Street., the Tom Rudolph Orchestra, and the Robert Durant Quartet. Personal honors include *Who's Who in America* and "Outstanding Young Men in America," and he was nominated three times for "Who's Who among American Teachers." He is a recipient of the Domenick Recchiuti award and multiple Haverford Township School District Education Foundation Teacher Tribute awards for excellence in teaching.

Sean Grier teaches choral music at the Durham School of the Arts (DSA) in Durham, North Carolina. He is currently one of three choral teachers on faculty at the DSA. Sean is a National Board Certified Teacher and holds degrees in Music Education and Vocal Performance from Michigan State University. During his time at DSA, Sean's choirs have performed across the United States and in Europe. His groups have collaborated with the Fisk Jubilee Singers, Eric Whitacre, Gwyneth Walker, and a variety of professional musicians and performers. Sean's main passion within the choral music education profession is cultivating and empowering male singers at the middle school and early high school levels.

Michelle Limor Herring recently completed her Ph.D. in Music Education at the University of North Texas in Denton and is currently an Assistant Professor of Music Education at Columbus State University in Columbus, Georgia. She previously earned a bachelor's degree in music studies from the University of Texas at Austin and a master's degree in Music Education from the University of North Texas. Michelle taught middle school choir for eight years in her hometown of Austin, Texas. Her choirs consistently received superior ratings in festivals and contests during her tenure, as well as many opportunities to perform with community choruses and religious organizations. Michelle was awarded campus "Teacher of the Year" in 2009. She has presented at state and national conventions and published in music education journals. She is inspired to discover innovative instructional strategies for teaching diverse student populations using music as a catalyst for learning, connecting, and motivating students of all backgrounds.

David Hirschorn has been a choral and guitar teacher for twenty-six years. He holds degrees from the University of Miami and Florida State University, a Ph.D. from Georgia State University, and is nationally board-certified. He wrote the guitar curriculum for the school district of Cobb County, Georgia and co-wrote the Georgia Performance Standards for middle school choruses. His choir at Durham Middle School performed at the 2008 Georgia Music Educator's Association (GMEA) convention, and he conducted both the 2009 GMEA District XIII Middle School Mixed Honor Choir and the 2012 GMEA District VII Middle School Treble Chorus. At Durham Middle School he teaches four choirs, guitar ensemble, and two semester-long guitar classes.

Michael Lehman is currently the codirector of bands at Evanston Township High School (ETHS) in Evanston, Illinois. Prior to beginning at ETHS, Michael was the Director of Bands at Edison Middle School in Champaign, IL (2006–2013). He earned his bachelor's and master's degrees in Music Education from the University of Illinois under the mentorship of Joe Manfredo and studied saxophone performance with Debra Richtmeyer and Ron Bridgewater. Mr. Lehman has been awarded six "Citations of Excellence" awards from the National Band Association and is an active clinician and guest conductor in the central Illinois area. He has served as the Illinois Music Education Association District 3 Junior High School Jazz Band Chairman for the past several years.

Marsha Miller (a pseudonym) completed her Master of Music Education degree and continues to teach band at Philip East Middle School in Illinois.

Andrew Nickles is now into his thirteenth year of teaching in the Tucson Unified Schools. He currently teaches at Gridley Middle School where he has integrated his string orchestras with his guitar ensembles; they perform his arrangements of rock, pop, country, and metal artists on top of traditional classical repertoire. Andrew's passion for tango, teaching, and linguistics coalesced as a cello student on a Rotary scholarship in Belgium as a young adult. From there he eventually attended college at the

University of Arizona in Tucson, Arizona, where he completed degrees in Cello Performance and French.

After becoming the youngest member of the Tucson Symphony Orchestra, Andrew continued to hone his teaching skills for Dennis Bourret's youth orchestras, the Tucson Junior Strings, as well as his private cello students Mr. Nickles completed his master's degree in Cello Performance at the University of Illinois.

Returning to Tucson, Andrew's interest in developing young string players on a daily basis grew, so he became a public school music teacher. He continues to perform his cello alongside Steinway artist Oscar Macchioni with their ensemble, Piazzolla da Camera. The tango ensemble recently played a recital at the prestigious St. Martin-in-the-Fields hall in London and in fall 2015 launched a four-city tour in Thailand. On the weekends, Andrew also enjoys playing electric bass for his rock/blues band, Priority One: Tucson, where they play for charities and local restaurants.

Gretchen Pearson finished her bachelor's degree in music from Eastern Illinois University (EIU) in 2006 and earned her master's degree in music education from the University of Illinois Urbana-Champaign in 2011. She also completed Suzuki Teacher Training from the University of Wisconsin–Stevens Point.

From 2003 to 2014, Gretchen worked as a private violin and viola teacher at the Champaign Suzuki Rolland program in the Conservatory of Central Illinois, the Aurora Suzuki Violin program, the West Suburban Suzuki Strings Group, and finally her own home studio. After graduating from EIU, Gretchen worked as an orchestra teacher at Indian Prairie School District #204 in Naperville, Illinois from 2007 to 2013. Since 2013, Gretchen has been teaching elementary and middle school orchestra at Community Consolidated School District 181 in Hinsdale, Illinois.

Kate Tyler (pseudonym) teaches middle school general music and choir in Illinois, and is one of the founding sponsors of her school's Gay-Straight Alliance. She holds a bachelor's and a master's degree in music education from the University of Illinois at Urbana-Champaign and has studied Education Through Music with the Richards Institute for seven years. She performs and directs community theatre and sings with local ensembles, including church choir.

Tavia Zerman continues to teach band at Hayes Middle School in Grand Ledge, Michigan. She is currently in her sixteenth year of teaching.

NOTES

CHAPTER 1

1. I will not get into the specifics of the mental and emotional ramifications of voice change for singers here because this book is intended for a broad audience of music teachers. However, see the Resources section for suggested reading on adolescent female and male voice change.

CHAPTER 2

1. The instructional strategy of ICE (ideas, connections, and extensions) is about teaching subject matter beyond the basic building blocks of vocabulary and small facts and making it meaningful for students on a number of levels. See the Resources section for more information.
2. According to their website, "Little Kids Rock is a national nonprofit organization that transforms children's lives by restoring and revitalizing music education in disadvantaged public schools." http://www.littlekidsrock.org/

CHAPTER 5

1. See http://www.merriam-webster.com/dictionary/humanity.
2. It should be said at the forefront that throughout my dissertation time with Deb, she remained incredibly humble about her own teaching and methodologies. In reality she struggled with how the project felt "terrifically narcissistic" and repeatedly commented that, "I have so much to be humble about." But for her, the bottom line is that music is a medium through which she works to teach adolescents about themselves and their place in the world. Everything else is a bonus.
3. The 1993 version of this book is no longer in print; however, there are 2002, 2007, and 2013 available editions of this book.

REFERENCES

Apatow, J. (Producer), & Mottola, G. (Director). 2007. *Superbad* [Motion picture]. USA: Columbia Pictures.

Arthur Ashe Learning Center. 2009. *Arthur Ashe: In His Words* (February 10). Retrieved from http://www.arthurashe.org/in-his-words.html

Banks, J. A. 1996. "The Canon Debate, Knowledge Construction, and Multicultural Education." In J. A. Banks, ed., *Multicultural Education, Transformative Knowledge, and Action: Historical and Contemporary Perspectives*, 3–39. New York: Teachers College Press.

Bennett, P. D., and D. R. Bartholomew. 1997. *SongWorks 1: Singing in the Education of Children*. Belmont, CA: Wadsworth.

Berk, R. A. 2002. *Humor as an Instructional Defibrillator*. Sterling, VA: Stylus.

Berk, R. A., and J. R. Nanda. 1998. "Effects of Jocular Instructional Methods on Attitudes, Anxiety, and Achievement in Statistics Courses." *Humor: International Journal of Humor Research* 11, no. 4: 383–409.

Blair, G. M., and R. S. Jones. 1965. *Psychology of Adolescence for Teachers*. New York: Macmillan.

Boostrom, R. 1997. "'Unsafe Spaces': Reflections on a Specimen of Educational Jargon." Opinion paper presented at the Annual Meeting of the American Educational Research Association, Chicago, March.

Boostrom, R. 1998. "'Safe Spaces': Reflections on an Educational Metaphor." *Journal of Curriculum Studies* 30, no. 4: 397–408.

Boyd, D. 2014. *It's Complicated: The Social Lives of Networked Teens*. London: Yale University Press.

Bronk, K. C. 2008. "Early Adolescents' Conceptions of the Good Life and the Good Person." *Adolescence* 43, no. 172: 713–732.

Brooks, R. B. 1991. *The Self-Esteem Teacher: Seeds of Self-Esteem*. Loveland, OH: Treehaus Communications.

Brooks, R. B. 1999. "Creating a Positive School Climate: Strategies for Fostering Self-Esteem, Motivation, and Resilience." In J. Cohen, ed., *Educating Minds and Hearts: Social Emotional Learning and the Passage into Adolescence*, 6–73. Alexandria, VA: Association for Supervision and Curriculum Development.

Carter, B. A. 2011. "A Safe Education for All: Recognizing and Stemming Harassment in Music Classes and Ensembles." *Music Educators Journal* 97, no. 4: 2–32.

Clandinin, D. J. & Connelly, F. M. 1995. *Teachers' Professional Knowledge Landscapes*. New York, NY: Teachers College Press.

Cottere, J. 2007. *Social Networks in Youth and Adolescence*. 2nd ed. New York: Routledge.

Crotty, M. 1998. *The Foundations of Social Research: Meaning and Perspective in the Research Process*. London: Sage.

Curwin, R. L., A. N. Mendler, and B. D. Mendler. 2008. *Discipline with Dignity*. 3rd ed. Alexandria, VA: Association for Supervision and Curriculum Development.

Cushman, K., and L. Rogers. 2008. *Fires in the Middle School Bathroom: Advice for Teachers from Middle Schoolers*. New York: New Press.

Csikszentmihalyi, M., and J. McCormack. 1986. "The Influence of Teachers." *Phi Delta Kappan* 67, no.(6): 415–419.

Daly, J. & Anspaugh, D. 1986. *Hoosiers* [Motion picture]. USA: De Haven Productions.

Darling-Hammond, L., J. French, and S. P. Garcia-Lopez. 2002. *Learning to Teach for Social Justice*. New York: Teachers College Press.

Davies, A. P., and M. J. Apter. 1980. "Humour and Its Effect on Learning in Children." In P. E. McGhee and A. J. Chapman, eds., *Children's Humour*, 23–253. Chichester: John Wiley & Sons.

Deak, J., and T. Deak. 2013. *The Owner's Manual for Driving Your Adolescent Brain*. San Francisco: Little Pickle Press.

Editors of Conari Press. 1993. *Random Acts of Kindness*. Berkeley, CA: self-published by author.

Editors of Conari Press. 2013. *Random Acts of Kindness: Then and Now*. Berkeley, CA: self-published by author.

Elkind, D. 1967. "Egocentrism in Adolescence." *Child Development* (38): 1025–34.

Ellison, P. T., and M. W. Reiches. 2012. "Puberty." In N. Cameron and B. Bogin, eds., *Human Growth and Development*, 81–107. 2nd ed. London: Elsevier.

Fostaty Young, S. 2005. "Teaching, Learning, and Assessment in Higher Education: Using ICE to Improve Student Learning." *Proceedings of the Improving Student Learning Symposium, London, UK* 13 (September): 105–15.

Fostaty Young, S., and R. J. Wilson. 1995. *Assessment and Learning: The ICE Approach*. Winnipeg, Manitoba: Portage & Main Press.

Frazzetto, G. 2013. *Joy, Guilt, Anger, Love: What Neuroscience Can—and Can't—Tell Us About How We Feel*. New York: Penguin.

Freire, P. 2005. *Teachers as Cultural Workers: Letters to Those Who Dare to Teach*. Boulder, CO: Westview Press.

Gay, Lesbian and Straight Education Network (GLSEN). n.d. *Four Steps Schools You Can Take to Create Safe Schools*. Retrieved from: http://www.glsen.org/article/four-steps-you-can-take-create-safe-schools

Gerber, T. 1994. "Nurturing the Young Adolescent: High Stakes for the School and Social Environment." In J. Hinckley, ed., *Music at the Middle Level: Building Strong Programs*, 5–12. Reston, VA: Music Educators National Conference.

Germanotta, S. & Laursen, J. 2011. Born This Way [Recorded by Lady Gaga]. On *Born This Way* [CD]. Santa Monica, CA: Interscope Records.

Giedd, J., J. Blumenthal, N. O. Jeffries, F. X. Castellanos, H. Liu, A. Zijdenbos, T. Paus, A. C. Evans, and J. L. Rapoport. 1999. "Brain Development during Childhood and Adolescence: A Longitudinal MRI Study." *Nature Neuroscience* 2: 861–63.

Gladstein, J. 2001. "Using Critical Questioning to Investigate Identity, Culture, and Difference." In W. Goodman, ed., *Living (and Teaching) in an Unjust World: New Perspectives on Multicultural Education*, 182–94. Portsmouth, NH: Heinemann.

Goodman, W. 2001. "Living (and Teaching) in an Unjust World." In W. Goodman (Ed.), *Living (and Teaching) in an Unjust World: New Perspectives on Multicultural Education*, 1–25). Portsmouth, NH: Heinemann.

Gross, S. 2013. "That's SO Gay: How to Address Homophobia in Schools." Presentation at the University of Illinois at Urbana-Champaign, March.

Gurian, S., & Stevens, K. 2011. *Boys and Girls Learn Differently! A Guide for Teachers and Parents*. San Francisco: Jossey-Bass.

Hastie, P. A. 1998. "Effect of Instructional Context of Teacher and Student Behaviors in Physical Education." *Journal of Classroom Interaction* 33, no. 2: 24–31.

Hickey, M. 2012. *Music outside the Lines: Ideas for Composing in K-12 Music Classrooms*. New York: Oxford University Press.

Hill, D. J. 1988. *Humor in the Classroom*. Springfield, IL: Charles C. Thomas.

Holley, L. C., and S. Steiner. 2005. "Safe Space: Student Perspectives on Classroom Environment." *Journal of Social Work Education* 41, no. 1: 49–64.

Howe, D. 2013. *Empathy: What It Is and Why It Matters*. New York: Palgrave Macmillan.

Howe, J. 2001. *The Misfits*. New York: Atheneum Books for Young Readers.

Humanity. (n.d.). In *Merriam-Webster online*. Retrieved from http://www.merriam-webster.com/dictionary/humanity.

Huttenlocher, P. 2002. *Neural Plasticity: The Effects of the Environment on the Development of the Cerebral Cortex*. Cambridge, MA: Harvard University Press.

Jersild, A. T. 1968. *The Psychology of Adolescence*. 2nd ed. New York: Macmillan.

Johnson, G. L. 2013. The *Hoosiers* Archive: FAQ. Retrieved from http://hoosiersarchive.com/trivia-4/faq/.

Kluth, P., and K. P. Colleary. 2002. "'Talking about Inclusion Like It's for Everyone': Sexual Diversity and the Inclusive Schooling Movement." In R. M. Kissen, ed., *Getting Ready for Benjamin: Preparing Teachers for Sexual Diversity in the Classroom*, 105–18). Lanham, MD: Rowman & Littlefield.

Kottler, J. A., and E. Kottler. 2007. *Counseling Skills for Teachers: Listening, Questioning, Modeling, Reframing, Goal Setting, Empathizing*. 2nd ed. Thousand Oaks, CA: Corwin Press.

Kuhn, D. 2009. "Adolescent Thinking." In R. M. Lerner and L. D. Steinberg, eds., *Handbook of Adolescent Psychology*, 1:152–86. 3rd ed. Hoboken, NJ: John Wiley & Sons.

Ladson-Billings, G. 2009. *The Dreamkeepers: Successful Teachers of African American Children*. San Francisco: Jossey-Bass.

Lafond, N. 2015. School Board to Vote on Naming Library for Vickers-Shelley. *The News-Gazette*. January 26. Retrieved from http://www.news-gazette.com/news/local/2015-01-26/school-board-vote-naming-library-vickers-shelley.html.

Lee, H. 1960. *To Kill a Mockingbird*. Philadelphia: J. B. Lippincott.

Levitin, D. J. 2006. *This Is Your Brain on Music: The Science of a Human Obsession*. New York: Plume.

Malin, H., T. S. Teilly, B. Quinn, and S. Moran. 2013. "Adolescent Purpose Development: Exploring Empathy, Discovering Roles, Shifting Priorities, and Creating Pathways. *Journal of Research on Adolescence* 24, no. 1: 186–99.

Martin, R. A. 2007. *The Psychology of Humor*. London: Elsevier.

Maslow, A. H. 1943. "A Theory of Human Motivation." *Psychological Review* 50: 370–96.

McMahan, I. 2008. *Adolescence*. New Jersey: Pearson.

Nelms, J. 2001. "A Descriptive Analysis of the Uses and Functions of Sarcasm in the Classroom Discourse of Higher Education." Unpublished doctoral dissertation, University of Florida, Gainesville.

Nelson, C. A., K. M. Thomas, and M. de Hann. 2006. "Neural Bases of Cognitive Development." In D. Kuhn, R. S. Siegler, W. Damon, and R. M. Lerner, eds. *Cognition, Perception, and Language: Handbook of Child Psychology*, 2:3–57. 6th ed. Hoboken, NJ: Wiley.

Novak, B. J. 2014. *One More Thing: Stories and Other Stories*. New York: Knopf Doubleday.

Patton, M. Q. 2002. *Qualitative Research and Evaluation Methods*. 3rd ed. Thousand Oaks, CA: Sage.

Paus, T. 2009. "Brain Development." In R. M. Lerner and L. D. Steinberg, eds., *Handbook of Adolescent Psychology*, 1:95–115. 3rd ed. New Jersey: John Wiley & Sons.

Perlstein, L. 2003. *Not Much Just Chillin': The Hidden Lives of Middle Schoolers*. New York: Ballantine.

Perry, K., Eriksen, M. S., Harnansen, T. E., Wilhelm, S., Dean, E. 2010. Firework [Recorded by Katy Perry]. On *Teenage Dream* [CD]. Los Angeles, CA: Capitol Records.

Raiber, M., and D. Teachout. 2014. *The Journey from Music Student to Teacher: A Professional Approach*. New York: Taylor & Francis.

Reasoner, R. W., and G. S. Dusa. 1991. *Building Self-Esteem in the Secondary School*. Palo Alto, CA: Consulting Psychologists Press.

Regelski, T. 2004. *Teaching General Music in Grades 4–8*. New York: Oxford University Press.

Riddle, D. 1994. "Attitudes Towards Differences: The Riddle Scale." In *Alone No More: Developing a School Support System for Gay, Lesbian and Bisexual Youth*, Minnesota State Dept. of Education, St. Paul, 32–33. Atlanta: Centers for Disease Control (DHHS), Atlanta, GA.

Rosenberg, M. 2003. *Nonviolent Communication: A Language of Life*. Encinitas, CA: Puddledancer Press.

Rubinstein, G. 2011. *Beyond Survival: How to Thrive in Middle and High School for Beginning and Improving Teachers*. New York: McGraw-Hill.

Salinger, J.D. 1951. *The Catcher in the Rye*. New York: Little, Brown and Company.

Sensoy, Ö., and R. DiAngelo. 2012. *Is Everyone Really Equal?: An Introduction to Key Concepts in Social Justice Education*. New York: Teachers College Press.

Snow, S. 2009. *Choral Conducting/Teaching: Real World Strategies for Success*. DVD. Available from www.giamusic.com.

Springer, S. and K. Persiani. 2011. *The Organized Teacher's Guide to Classroom Management*. New York: McGraw-Hill.

Strauch, B. 2003. *The Primal Teen: What the New Discoveries about the Brain Tell Us about Our Kids*. New York: Doubleday.

Strong, T. 2013. "The Culture of Humour in the Classroom: The Good, the Bad, and the Other." *Canadian Music Educator*, 54, no.4: 31–33.

Sweet, B. M. 2003. "Personal and Environmental Factors That Influence Sixth and Seventh Grade Students' Determinations of Whether to Remain in Choir." Unpublished master's thesis, Michigan State University, East Lansing.

Sweet, B. M. 2008. "Everybody's Somebody in My Class: A Case Study of an Exemplary Middle School Choir Teacher." Unpublished doctoral dissertation, Michigan State University, East Lansing.

Sweet, B. 2010. "A Case Study: Middle School Boys' Perceptions of Singing and Participation in Choir." In *Update: Applications of Research in Music Education* 28: 5–12.

Tanner, J. M. 1972. "Sequence, Tempo, and Individual Variation in Growth and Development of Boys and Girls Aged Twelve to Sixteen." In J. Kagan and R. Coles, eds., *Twelve to Sixteen: Early Adolescence*. New York: Norton.

Teaching Tolerance. n.d. "Developing Empathy: Middle grades (Lesson plan)." Retrieved from http://www.tolerance.org/supplement/developing-empathy-middle-grades.

Teaching Tolerance. n.d. "Someone Else's Shoes (Lesson plan)." Retrieved from http://www.tolerance.org/sites/default/files/general/someone%20else's%20shoes.pdf.

This I Believe. *The Original Invitation from This I Believe*. Retrieved from http://thisibelieve.org/history/invitation/.

Thomas, M., and M. Johnson. 2008. New Advances in Understanding Sensitive Periods in Brain Development. *Current Directions in Psychological Science* 17: 1–5.

Toulis, J. 2011. "Teaching Children Empathy." In A. N. Johnson and M. W. Neagley, eds., *Educating from the Heart: Theoretical and Practical Approaches to Transforming Education*. Lanham, MD: Rowman & Littlefield Education.

Tyink, S. 2008. "Teaching Empathy to Young Adolescents: Suggestions for Building Empathy in the Middle Grades (Developmental Designs article). January. Retrieved from http://www.originsonline.org/newsletters/winter-2008-dd/teaching-empathy-young-adolescents.

University of Oregon. n.d. *Teaching Effectiveness Program (TEP)*. Retrieved from tep.uoregon.edu.

Vaid, J. 2002. "Humor and Laughter." In R. G. Morris and C. L. Worsley, eds., *Encyclopedia of the Human Brain*, 505–16. London: Elsevier.

van den Berg, O. 2001. "Affirming Difference While Building a Nation: Teaching Diversity in Neo-Apartheid America." In W. Goodman, ed., *Living (and Teaching) in an Unjust World: New Perspectives on Multicultural Education*, 150–61. Portsmouth, NH: Heinemann.

Veatch, T. C. 1998. "A Theory of Humor." *HUMOR: International Journal of Humor Research* 11: 161–215.

Vermond, K. 2013. *Growing Up Inside and Out*. Toronto, ON: Owlkids Books.

Wiggins, G., and J. McTighe. 2006. *Understanding by Design*. 2nd ed. Upper Saddle River, New Jersey: Pearson Education.

Wink, J. 2001. "Finding the Freedom to Teach and Learn, and Live." In W. Goodman, ed., *Living (and Teaching) in an Unjust World: New Perspectives on Multicultural Education*, 208–16. Portsmouth, NH: Heinemann.

Woodford, P. G. 2005. *Democracy and Music Education: Liberalism, Ethics, and the Politics of Practice*. Bloomington: Indiana University Press.

Zaichkowsky, L. D., and G. A. Larson. 1995. "Physical, Motor, and Fitness Development in Children and Adolescents." *Journal of Education* 177, no. 2: 55–79.

Ziegler, V., G. Boardman, and M. D. Thomas. 1985. "Humor, Leadership, and School Climate." *Clearing House* 58: 346–48.

INDEX

CPSIA information can be obtained
at www.ICGtesting.com
Printed in the USA
BVHW031343240621
609769BV00005B/25

9 780199 372072